THE RED
MONARCH

 W · W · NORTON & COMPANY · NEW YORK

THE RED MONARCH

Scenes from the Life of Stalin

— — —

YURI KROTKOV

TRANSLATED BY TANYA E. MAIRS

EDITED BY CAROL HOUCK SMITH

Copyright © 1979 by W. W. Norton & Company, Inc.
Published simultaneously in Canada by George J. McLeod Limited, Toronto.
Printed in the United States of America
All Rights Reserved
First Edition

Book design by Antonina Krass
Typefaces used are v.i.p. Times Roman and typositor Windsor Light Condensed
Manufactured by Vail-Ballou Press, Inc.

Library of Congress Cataloging in Publication Data
Krotkov, Yuri
The red monarch.
1. Stalin, Josif, 1879–1953.   2. Heads of state— Russia—Scenes from his life.
I. Mairs, Tanya E.; Smith, Carol Houck.   II. Title.
DK268.S8K74   1979   947.084'2092'4 [B] 78–12127
ISBN 0–393–08836–7

1 2 3 4 5 6 7 8 9 0

Contents

5

— CONTENTS —

From the Author

This is not another biography of Stalin, nor is it an academic essay or memoir by someone who was Stalin's relative or bodyguard. I never met Stalin and I never talked to him. But for thirty-five years I lived with this man, day and night, voluntarily and involuntarily, thinking about him and knowing that my destiny depended on him and his political reasoning. Actually, all of this came about because I was Stalin's contemporary.

His image was, and is, forever imprinted on me.

In this book I have tried to depict this image of Stalin, bearing in mind that he was not only a dictator, but also a human being. In other words, I have tried to revive my past as well as the most typical circumstances of the so-called Stalin era, making Stalin himself talk and act the way that he did, in my view. Of course, I could not do this without relying on my literary imagination, my temperament, and my intuition. In some instances, I even felt I had to change historical events slightly and to shift dates and details a bit,

7

hoping at the same time that this would not take me too far from the truth.

For example, it is historically true that a few months before Stalin's death the chief of his bodyguards, General Vlasek, who had held this position for many years, was fired. However, in the episode "Death" I "saved" him until the leader's last day. You may ask why I did this. I wanted to give Vlasek a chance to portray the end of Stalin, to portray it not only as a factual happening, but also with a pinch of exaggeration, adding all those particulars that only Vlasek would know about his long-time master and the others. And, of course, Vlasek would reveal his own psychological state of mind. In my view, this episode could not have been vivid enough if—instead of the colorful General Vlasek—I had used another KGB man, Khrustalyev, who became Stalin's chief of bodyguards for a short time after Vlasek.

Many years ago a friend in Moscow said:

"It seems to me that Stalin is a gardener who persistently tries to open rosebuds with his clumsy fingers, not content to wait until they are opened by nature."

It was a sharp symbolic image. In writing this book I often felt the necessity to resort to this kind of symbolic interpretation; as a result, in some episodes, something that began as quite realistic was transformed and brought to the edge of the grotesque.

Probably it is fair to say that this is a book about Stalin written in fictional form. Yes, it is fiction. However, it is also a documentary. I strongly believe in it because my imagination, my temperament, and my intuition were constantly controlled by first-hand knowledge and by that strict and intensively saturated witness—my conscience.

I set out to write a book in which Stalin would come to life the way he was, or rather the way he appeared and appears now to me: good and bad, great and ordinary, principled and unprincipled; a man with many deep-rooted contradictions; a man who even now is considered an enigma; a man who dominated an era and who was dominated by it; a man who instilled fear in a whole people and who himself lived in fear; a man who was powerful, ambitious, cruel, heartless, and crude; and a man who was kind, gentle, modest, and charming, with a tragic family life; he was a Georgian with traits found only among Georgians; he was shrewd and arrogant; he was a man whom some considered a true Leninist and believing Marxist and others a charlatan and criminal.

Now a few words about myself and the material I used. A Russian, I was born in Soviet Georgia, and from earliest childhood was brought up among Georgians. I studied Georgian in school, I sang Georgian songs, I ate Georgian dishes and drank Georgian wines. Before I joined the Moscow Literary Institute, I lived in Tbilisi, the capital of Soviet Georgia, which I love as my motherland even today. The fact of my birth gave me the advantage of feeling that I was almost a Georgian, and later opened a door for me into the circle of Georgian intelligentsia and top-ranking Soviet and party officials in Moscow. In confidence, they told me many interesting and unique things about Stalin, which no ordinary Soviet citizen could know. I collected those stories and details and stored them in my memory. In addition, I was acquainted with a well-known Georgian actor, Gelovani, who played Stalin in many Soviet movies depicting the Great Leader. Gelovani had met Stalin, he had the opportunity to study materials that were available only to him, and he was honest and open with me, sometimes making fun of Stalin. It was he who told me about the historic supper with Stalin that I reproduced satirically in the episode in this book called "Two Stalins."

So I believe that the facts here are in the *spirit* of reality. Otherwise they would have been rejected by my time-locator, with its thirty-five-year record.

In 1963 I left Moscow for London. At the time I was with others in the Soviet tourist delegation as a well-established Moscow dramatist. But then I did not return to the USSR. From the start of my life in exile I began to write about Stalin, and I continued to do so all the years that followed. This process became an absolute part of me, as if I had to confirm that I was not an "ungrateful descendant" of Stalin.

In justifying my reason for writing another book about Stalin, I think this is about all I have to say. Of course, I hope that my attempt is completely different from other books published in the West during the last two or three decades, and I hope it will have its own merit.

Now let me introduce my protagonist—Josif Vissarionovich Stalin.

Yuri Krotkov

June 1978

THE RED
MONARCH

Mekhlis, Tea!

At night he could not sleep. As always his left arm, which was shorter than the right and seemed to hang limply from his shoulder, bothered him. His sleep was fretful. His mouth was dry and his heart beat rapidly. And his dream was one he had had before, which made it even more senseless and frightening.

Two enormous Great Danes were chewing ferociously at his feet. He felt no pain, but he did feel an overwhelming impotence at not being able to stop them. He and the dogs were on the pebble-covered shore of the Liakhva River, near his native town, Gori. But the river flowed backward, although the rocks that rose from the water were as he had remembered them from his childhood: dark blue, steep, and smooth.

Now the road to Moscow, surrounded by pine forests, seemed gloomy. He sat in the back of the Packard in his usual corner and, as he looked at the thick neck of the chauffeur, he thought how unpleasant it was that behind

him and in front there were several more cars with bodyguards. Muscovites called them the "Stalin cavalcade."

He took a deep breath. In memory he returned to the
Liakhva River. Now, of course, it flowed as it had for a
thousand years, into the Kura. Oh, how many happy days
he had spent in his youth on this river, swimming in its
turbulent waters, climbing on its rocks with his schoolmates, playing children's games! He remembered how
once, on the shore of the Liakhva, his schoolmates had almost crucified him because they thought he had been involved in a theft. He had been innocent, but it was a good
thing that the huge, kind-hearted Rodion Chikvidze, the son
of the local deacon, had stood up for him. If he hadn't,
things would have gone badly.

It was then that Stalin became friends with Rodion, went
to his house, started going to church more often. He lost
track of his friend, however, when he moved to Tiflis* and
entered the seminary. Some time afterward, already in the
Soviet period, someone told him that Chikvidze had become involved in political activity and was secretary of the
regional committee of the Communist party somewhere in
Georgia. Stalin thought that he should look up Rodion but
time never permitted this, for he was already the secretary
general of the Central Committee of the Soviet Communist
party.

As he sat in the Packard on the way to Moscow, the
thought of Rodion Chikvidze somehow frightened him and
an ominous premonition arose within him.

Later, as Stalin was going into his private room, past the
office of Mekhlis, the chief of secretariat stood up and said
as always:

---

*Tiflis is the old name for Tbilisi, the capital of Soviet Georgia.

"Good day, Josif Vissarionovich." Mekhlis was a tall stately Jew with a handsome face and curly hair.

Stalin nodded and said casually, "Greetings."

Leaving the door ajar, he approached his desk. On the glass surface lay a big blue file with all the current business of the secretary general prepared by Mekhlis and his staff.

Stalin lit his pipe, threw the match on the floor, then unbuttoned the collar of his khaki-colored jacket, and sat down. He liked this desk, the black telephones, the inkwell on the marble top, and all the other things. He smoked for another moment or two, for he knew that the chief of the secretariat would under no circumstances enter, even with important and pressing business. This smart Jew understood that Stalin needed a half hour at least to look through the confidential summary of Tass (Telegraph Agency of the Soviet Union), to make two or three phone calls, consider immediate business—in other words, time in which to enter his working trance.

The sun shone through the window. The ridges of the Kremlin wall could be seen. On the wall, the big clock set in walnut quietly measured eternity.

Stalin procrastinated. He did not want to open the blue file. His left arm bothered him and his mouth was dry again. He thought that he really should muster up the strength and give up smoking. Even his doctors recommended it. Finally, he set aside his pipe, put his elbows on the glass top, and opened the file.

First of all, there was the list of the "enemies of the people" who were to be shot on the recommendation of Ezhov, the people's commissar of internal affairs. Twenty-six names were on the list—a pillar of the dead. These people, according to Ezhov, were acting against Stalin, that is, against the Soviet state.

He had to look through this list, cross out or add names, and "seal the document"—that is, sign it in the left-hand corner. After this the document would go to the Politburo and be signed by every member without exception. But Stalin knew full well that that was only a formality; his signature was the deciding one. He knew that only he sentenced, that the rest were only witnesses, like the hooting crowd surrounding the hangman.

He skimmed through the list and stopped at number twenty-four: Rodion Chikvidze. The same Rodion whom Stalin had recalled on the journey from his *dacha* to Moscow; the same who in essence had saved his life on the shores of the Liakhva.

He must call Ezhov and ask him about the crime committed by Chikvidze. But he didn't. He stood up, lit his pipe again, and started pacing up and down the room. That was his favorite habit: to go from one end to the other. It was so good for thinking. Since morning he had not been able to rid himself of that premonition about Rodion, and now on the table there was this list with Rodion's name on it. His premonition did not appear to be for nothing.

Stalin was not religious. On the contrary, atheism had led him to Marxism. And all this despite the fact that his mother, Keke, was known in Gori to have been a near religious fanatic. Stalin, however, had been superstitious all his life, although he took pains to conceal it.

Are there, then, otherworldly and mystical forces on earth even though they are hidden in dreams? It couldn't have been mere coincidence that he saw the Liakhva River in his dreams, and that it was flowing backward. Nor was it coincidence that this dream had led him to think of Rodion Chikvidze.

A chain of coincidences.

He was irritated that the force that he felt pressing on him could not be explained away by a system of philosophical postulates, that he could not subject it to his logic, and that it twisted him about like a marionette. He knew that he had to return to the table and cross out with a red pencil the name of his childhood friend from the "enemies of the people" list, condemned to be shot. He knew that his Georgian heart commanded him to do that and that he could not overcome his own human nature. In his heart he was convinced that he was too kind and soft a person. He even reproached himself for this. But in his position, as the party leader, it was necessary to be absolutely pitiless. The future of the entire world was balanced on the scales of history. What if this Rodion was a traitor to Marxism and had become a renegade? What if he had said somewhere that Stalin was a tyrant and a murderer? What if he supported Trotsky?

When there had been talk about his closest comrade, Sergo Orzhonikidze, also a Georgian, Stalin had not hesitated and had not given in to sentimentality, this despite the fact that he was convinced that Sergo undoubtedly would put a bullet into his own head after their last discussion—which, in fact, Sergo had done.

No, it was not easy to sign Rodion Chikvidze's death warrant. That premonition had shuffled the cards and added something uncontrollable. It drove one out of the realm of reality and paralyzed the will. What kind of deviltry was this! The Russian satirist Gogol wrote about such things. But Stalin did not like Gogol very much.

The list of the condemned lay on the desk, and awaited the approval of the leader.

In despair, Stalin admitted to his own helplessness. He

could not understand what was happening to him. Perhaps the years were taking their toll. But, he had only turned sixty. At this age, other government leaders were just getting started.

He had been capable of treating his own wife, whom he truly loved, mercilessly. Her suicide weighed on his conscience. He felt that probably in every two-legged creature there was a hidden self-negation, that each of us consists of two characters—if not three or five—and each lives with a constant conflict of ideas and will, that this is precisely the dialectical process within the individual, and it is this that separates human beings from animals.

Were there two Karl Marxes? Were there two Lenins? If there had been two Lenins, it was clear to Stalin that the cruel and heartless one had won. This Stalin knew from the time when he had worked with Lenin in the underground and during the first years of the Soviet regime.

So what if Lenin had been cruel and heartless? He, Stalin, was a Georgian, and he, Stalin, would decide to save Rodion Chikvidze. At this moment the weak side of Stalin's character dominated, the man for whom youth, friendship, and the past were still dear. And if he pardoned Rodion, who would know the real motive behind it? Would anyone dare to ask him about it?

Stalin sat down at the desk. All he had to do was pick up the red pencil and cross out number twenty-four.

At this very moment, however, his glance fell on a new button marked with the carefully written word "Tea." It was right next to the buzzer with which he summoned Mekhlis.

What nonsense! He could not believe his eyes. So that's it. Unquestionably an act of Mekhlis's.

The fact of the matter was that Stalin always drank tea during his working hours. Freshly brewed Georgian tea invigorated him. He liked it when Mekhlis brought tea in a glass, with a glass holder and a silver spoon. And for this reason Stalin usually left his office door ajar. He would raise his voice slightly and say:

"Mekhlis, tea!"

And in a few minutes Mekhlis would bring a glass of tea, place it on the desk in front of Stalin and respectfully say:

"Please, Josif Vissarionovich."

Mekhlis's deference, collectedness, and precision annoyed Stalin, but at the same time he needed exactly this type of assistant and in his heart he respected this Jew (to himself, he called him "my Jew").

Perhaps Mekhlis had decided that it would be easier for Stalin to push a button, instead of raising his voice to call, "Mekhlis, tea!" That day, prior to Stalin's arrival, a new buzzer must have been installed and connected to a bell in the special kitchen that served him.

If Mekhlis had done this in order to oblige him, that was one thing. But Mekhlis could have done it because he was tired of bringing Stalin tea, because he considered it beneath the dignity of the chief of the secretariat.

In Stalin's mind, the second theory was more plausible. And at this point he was seized with wrath. He flared up, without trying to control himself. Grabbing the button that said "Tea," he wrenched it to the side as hard as he could so that he would disconnect the wires. Not succeeding at first, he then took hold of the button with both hands and, this time with a wider swing, disconnected both button and wires. The palm of his hand hurt slightly. The veins on his forehead protruded. His lips turned white.

Stalin tossed the button and wires into the wastebasket. Then he lowered himself heavily into the chair.

Mekhlis, who was sitting in his own office, suddenly heard the loud "Mekhlis, tea!" from the other side of the door. And he understood that he had made a serious mistake when he had ordered the new button installed on the leader's desk without consulting Stalin. But, if he had tried to come to an agreement with Stalin in advance, nothing would have come of it. So Mekhlis had taken the risk. And he now realized that he had taken the risk for naught, and that as a result a difficult day awaited him. The leader would either sulk in anger, or he would make fun of Mekhlis by telling vulgar Jewish anecdotes.

"Mekhlis, tea!" The tone was loud and impatient.

Five minutes later, when Mekhlis brought Stalin a glass of tea, brewed the way Stalin liked, in the glass holder and with a silver spoon, he caught the near violent look on the leader's face. Stalin alone knew how to look at his subordinates in that way, with a slight frown in which something serpentlike was revealed. When Stalin was angry, he would stop talking. His eyes and twitching mustache spoke for him.

Mekhlis, deliberately and respectfully, as though nothing had happened, put the glass of tea on the desk and said:

"Please, Josif Vissarionovich."

In answer, Stalin gave him Ezhov's list on which number twenty-four remained in its place; it had not been crossed out, and in the upper left-hand corner of the document was the signature: J. Stalin.

As Mekhlis went from the desk to the door, he heard Stalin say.

"A dog deserves a dog's death."

That night, or rather toward morning, Stalin returned from the Kremlin to his *dacha*. In his dreams he saw again two enormous Great Danes, which again chewed ferociously at his feet. He did not feel any pain, but he felt painfully helpless in his efforts to stop them. Again he was on the shores of the Liakhva River, near his native village, Gori. And again the river flowed backward.

Thank You, Comrade Stalin

You can swear at him, you can all call him a tyrant and a bloodsucker, because he did indeed send several million people back to their great-grandfathers, but I personally must be grateful to him. It is, one could say, a historical paradox. He saved my life, literally. If it had not been for him, I would have rotted away in some concentration camp in the remote part of Siberia.

However, I should introduce myself, otherwise you will not understand anything.

I, Konstantin Gamsahurdia, was a famous novelist during the stormy years. I had written many epics. I probably surpassed even Honoré de Balzac. I will not hide the fact that all my books were historical. I did not write about the present, which I am afraid was not my genre. I uncovered the beauty of the past. It is true that czars appeared everywhere in my work. Without czars I could not have managed, because the past itself could not have managed without them. History in bygone days revolved around czars and

23

czarinas. My works were read during those stormy years and are being read today, too, I hope. We, the Georgians, are an odd people; all of us, the rich and the poor, are romantics, and in our hearts we are knights. We all love our past, particularly because it is inexhaustible. And what can you do if a thousand years ago servants loved their masters and never dreamed of revolution? That came later, and that, I am afraid, was not my genre.

But let me return to the subject. In 1937 or, to be more exact, beginning in 1937, there were general arrests in our beloved Georgia. Some called them "Stalin's incarcerations." Perhaps, historically, they were justified, but in human terms they were a terrible disaster. Almost all of my friends, Georgian prose writers and poets, were simply liquidated. And I will say honestly that during those years my wife and son and I went to bed with our clothes on, and my blanket and pillows were packed, because I expected to be arrested any night.

Nevertheless, I was not taken, and here is why:

It was by chance, most probably, that our great leader, Stalin, read one of my novels when he had moved from Moscow to the shores of the Black Sea for a rest. There in Esheri he had a magnificent *dacha,* a whole estate, in fact, which in former days belonged only to czars. And it was there, I repeat, that the leader read one of my novels. It was then that the young but balding Beria came to Esheri at Stalin's invitation. He was our big shot. In those days he occupied the position of first secretary of the Transcaucasian Committee of the Communist party, but he was already becoming Stalin's favorite.

And so, the leader and Beria were sitting on the veranda of Stalin's *dacha,* in wicker chairs, drinking Borzhom water and speaking in Georgian, because they did not particularly like Russian. The leader was wearing a white linen suit and boots, and Beria as usual was wearing a semimilitary uniform of khaki.

Stalin suddenly asked:

"What is what's-his-name Gamsahurdia doing now?"

"Which Gamsahurdia?" asked Beria, because in Georgia there were, and probably still are, at least two hundred persons with the same last name as mine. And all are, of course, distant relatives.

"The novelist," Stalin said.

"Ah." Beria looked watchfully at Stalin. "He's still alive, Josif Vissarionovich."

Stalin scratched his mustache and asked slowly:

"Is it true that he studied in Paris?"

"Yes," answered Beria, not having ascertained in which direction the leader was headed.

"They say he is eccentric. Yes?"

"Eccentric? What do you mean, Josif Vissarionovich, batono?"*

"I have heard, Beria, that he wears an old-fashioned Parisian hat, a coat with a long fur collar, a bow tie instead of a necktie, and that he has on his finger a ring with a valuable stone."

"That is true," answered Beria more confidently, since he had decided by this time that Stalin was criticizing me.

"And I heard that his boots are still from Paris, and he wears spats from time to time."

"About his spats, you're right, Josif Vissarionovich," said Beria. "I saw him in spats myself. In my opinion, he looked like a parrot."

"Why a parrot?"

*The Georgian word for sir or master.

"That is a very un-Soviet style," Beria answered.

I will say for myself that I actually had studied in Paris, and wore a felt hat and spats, and a ring on my little finger, but I assure you that I did not resemble a parrot.

The leader then asked:

"And does he speak French and German fluently?"

Beria nodded.

"Good. And what does he write, Beria, do you know?"

"Novels, batono, Josif Vissarionovich, many novels. All are about Georgian czars and czarinas."

"Aha!" Stalin scratched his mustache and, dragging out his words, said: "Does that mean he idealizes the past?"

"Yes," Beria answered, somewhat embarrassed.

"He extols all kinds of Czar Iraklievs and Czarina Tamaras," Stalin threw in with a sneer.

"He does," agreed Beria.

Stalin poured some Borzhom water into his glass and said, "While Lenin and I were creating the October Revolution. Who needs it? Who, Beria?"

"What do you mean, Josif Vissarionovich?" Beria asked carefully.

"Who needs what what's-his-name Gamsahurdia writes? I read one of his novels this week. And I will say honestly, if he had written this for children, then it is not very comprehensible, but if he wrote it for adults, then it is, in my opinion, harmful."

Here I am afraid I cannot agree with the great leader. First of all, he understood nothing about literature and was a poorly educated person, even though he had studied in a seminary and, alas, was later considered the highest expert in all phases of life: in science, in economics, in agriculture, and, of course, in art. Secondly, my novels were understood by children. So far as adults are concerned, then it is a question of taste and preference. In any case, all my books celebrate beauty and human kindness.

After Stalin had uttered the word *harmful,* Beria stood up. His pince-nez flashed with reflected light. "You are right, Josif Vissarionovich, batono, I have myself been thinking about that. Somehow I could never get my hands on that restorer of capitalism and monarchism. Censorship must be intensified, and we must take some administrative actions."

The leader understood that Beria had accepted his words as an order, and said:

"All right, but . . . don't you arrest him, which you know how to do so well."

Beria looked at his master with bewilderment. He knew full well that the initiator of mass repression in the Soviet Union was the leader himself, but Stalin acted as though he had nothing to do with it, as though arrests were made regardless of his will.

Stalin repeated:

"You can give him a working over in the newspapers, but don't arrest him, which you know how to do so well."

And I was not arrested, even though I idealized czars and czarinas. This was, I am afraid, my genre. Stalin himself defended me. For had he not uttered those last words, Beria would have called Bakhcho Kobulov (the executioner from state security) in Tbilisi, and an hour later I would no longer have been on this earth, or I would have been sitting behind bars awaiting exile.

You will ask why the Great Leader, who along with Lenin "created" the October Revolution, decided to save my life. I will give this answer: I think that he was basically a Georgian, regardless of the fact that he was the leader of the international proletariat. And every Georgian, as I have mentioned, rich or poor, in his heart still loves his past with its czars and czarinas. That is the kind of people we are, the Georgians.

You will of course ask how I learned about the Stalin-Beria chats concerning me. Believe it or not, from Beria himself, but after the death of our Great Leader. I then came to Moscow. Beria, as is known, had been transferred to the capital of the USSR by Stalin in 1938, and from that time on, almost without interruption, he headed the Soviet secret police. In a word, he was like the head gendarme in czarist days. Beria invited me to his *dacha* and there laid out his cards. I must admit that when I heard all of this from him, I involuntarily exclaimed:

"Thank you, Comrade Stalin!"

Beria burst out laughing and said:

"The old man was a scoundrel, the son of a bitch . . ."

In conclusion, if you were to ask me why Beria invited me to his *dacha* and why he laid out the cards for me, I would answer as follows: Beria himself was a first-class scoundrel, but he was also a Georgian, and in his heart I think he also loved our country with its czars and czarinas, that is, those times when servants adored their masters and did not dream of revolution. Of course, Beria did not read my novels and, in general, as marshal of the Soviet Union and as minister of internal affairs, he did not come in contact with books. That, I am afraid, was not his genre.

The Conference at Teheran

The State Committee of Defense decided that flying from Moscow to Teheran would be risky because the war was in full swing and the Germans still controlled the Soviet air corridors. Stalin, accompanied by his closest advisers and several members of the Politburo, went as far as Baku by train and then proceeded by automobile to Iran. Six government lounge cars and three cars carrying black limousines moved along between two armored railway cars equipped with additional antiaircraft guns. Stalin's party stopped only once, at night, at a deserted station that had been surrounded by troops in advance. For an hour the leader walked along the platform. The road from Baku to Teheran was bearable enough, and carefully guarded, because this was the second year that American Studebakers and Willises, carrying foodstuffs and supplies (in assistance to the USSR against Hitler) constantly traveled this way.

From the time he left Moscow for Baku, Stalin studied documents that described President Roosevelt and decided that he had to break through the Western bloc at all costs—that is, he had to try to separate Churchill and Roosevelt and woo the latter to his side. If only he could exert some influence on the American! Stalin could not stand the British prime minister. He called him "the bulldog" in private, and understood the fact that Churchill could swing 180 degrees at any moment; moreover, Stalin was informed that Churchill sometimes referred to him as "the Asian." Roosevelt seemed to him to be different, less complex and perhaps even naive; in addition, it was Roosevelt who had instituted major social reforms in the United States. America, in general, had interested Stalin for a long time, and, although he publicly attacked American monopolism, deep down inside he admired a country with unparalleled economic potential.

Stalin wore a new military uniform (especially sewn for this occasion) to the meeting with Roosevelt; he trimmed his mustache slightly and appeared confident, standing up straight without slouching.

The leader liked Roosevelt from first glance, primarily because of his luminous eyes and silky-gray, thinning hair. The president's face reminded him of his catechism teacher at the seminary, whom all the students liked; it was just as kind and pleasant. And the fact that this person was ill, with almost completely paralyzed legs, made him even more attractive to Stalin. The leader suddenly recalled someone else from his childhood, the old man Revaz, who sold cigarettes and matches on the main street of Gori, who was also paralyzed. Stalin, as a boy, often sat next to him, right on the sidewalk, and warmed himself in the sun.

Strangely enough, sick people always aroused a sense of compassion in Stalin. Most probably, this was a trait he inherited from his mother, Keke. She used to spend days and nights at the bedside of her neighbors when they were sick.

In the company of Roosevelt, the leader felt comfortable. He was animated, irresistibly witty, even though interpretation from Russian to English, and vice versa, was necessary. Stalin, who was usually quite rude and abrupt, in this case was amazingly considerate and courteous, and his manners did not betray his simple Georgian background. He carried himself simply and casually, for the leader could be charming if he chose to be.

But Stalin understood that one cannot get far on charm alone. Questions very important to the USSR were to be decided at this conference. The cold, cruel facts of politics were at work. And "the bulldog" was trying with all his might to trip things up, constantly hanging around the American president, and throwing out his caustic jokes about Soviet dictatorship.

The day after the meeting with Roosevelt, Stalin, early in the morning while shaving with his dangerous straight-edged razor and running it along his sharpening stone, suddenly thought of something that Shakespeare's Iago would have envied. It was risky, but it was in the style of the leader, for it could be used to his advantage.

He called for Beria, who was already a member of the State Committee of Defense, minister of internal affairs and state security, and ordered him to stage an attempt on President Roosevelt's life.

"What was that you said?" asked Beria.

"Everything has to be done, except for one thing," said Stalin. "He should not be killed. He can be useful to us. But stage a real attempt! Word should, of course, get to Germany, to Hitler. Suppose, Comrade Beria, that the secret service of that madman got wind of our meeting in Teheran and sent a group of his terrorists here.''

''I understand, Josif Vissarionovich.'' Beria was thinking that Stalin was a great sage and a great villain as well, and he frankly envied him.

''Everything will be done as ordered.''

''You have suitable people who speak German like Germans don't you? Give them the appropriate documents and weapons. And then at the last minute, arrest them. I need concrete evidence. I will have to tell Roosevelt about this. He will have to understand that it was our people who saved his life. Is that clear?''

Beria carried out the leader's orders exactly. Preparations for the attempt took a few hours and a great deal of energy, because this had to be done on Iranian territory and not Soviet, although the Soviet government then controlled life in this small country. In a word, the operation went smoothly, without a hitch. And nothing was leaked to the press.

In the evening Stalin requested an audience with Roosevelt, after informing him that there was something highly important that he had to convey personally. Roosevelt invited Stalin to his residence. And it was here that the leader told in full detail about the alleged attempt and how Soviet agents had warned him of it. All of this made a great impression on the American. He exacted several more details, and received exhaustive answers in each case. Roosevelt then said:

''Mr. Stalin, may I see the Soviet officer who headed the operation?''

''Of course, Mr. Roosevelt.''

The leader called Beria, and in half an hour the head of the operation, a certain Kravchenko, arrived. He was a tall man, about thirty-five years old, with a handsome Russian face and curly chestnut hair. In Hollywood, stars are made from people like this. He was elegantly dressed and spoke English perfectly.

"Here is the hero who saved your life Mr. President," Stalin said, pointing toward Kravchenko.

The interpreter translated Stalin's words, even though Kravchenko could have translated them himself. Roosevelt beckoned the Soviet officer to come toward him, and stared fixedly into his eyes. The American then asked Kravchenko some questions, and was struck not so much by the answers as by the Soviet officer's English, which showed almost no trace of accent. Roosevelt asked where Kravchenko was born; the latter answered that he was born on the Volga in the town of Saratov, and that he had finished secondary school there.

In conclusion, the American president shook Kravchenko's hand and said:

"Thank you, general."

The interpreter translated Roosevelt's words, and Stalin burst out laughing. The American did not understand, and looked bewildered. He also seemed puzzled by the fact that Kravchenko had turned red in the face and lost his composure.

Stalin twisted his mustache and said: "In your country, Mr. President, all kinds of commentators call Comrade Stalin a dictator. In wartime, power must be consolidated in the hands of one man. I therefore agree. I am a dictator. But you have just disproved that. Yes, *disproved*. A dictator has total power and of course in wartime awards military ranks. Nevertheless, you have just done that for me."

Roosevelt continued to look questioningly at Stalin.

"The fact of the matter is," continued the latter, "that Kravchenko was only a colonel several minutes ago. Now he is a general."

A smile appeared on the American's face.

"If that's the case, forgive me, I only thought that . . ."

"There is no need to apologize, Mr. President," Stalin said. "This is very good. I will award the rank of general to Colonel Kravchenko tomorrow. However," and here Stalin spoke directly to Kravchenko, "remember that the initiative in this matter came from Mr. Roosevelt. Remember and be proud of that, Comrade Kravchenko. It was an American president who promoted you to general. I am simply not objecting to it. Or, if you prefer, Kravchenko, then it is we, Mr. Roosevelt and I, who gave you the rank of general. Such things do not happen frequently in this world."

Roosevelt's bright eyes showed his appreciation that Stalin had transformed the matter into a joke.

He kept this incident secret. Not one word of the "attempt" on his life was leaked to the press. Perhaps he made this decision because he did not completely believe Stalin and Kravchenko.

As for Stalin, he returned to Moscow with the conviction that he had seduced the American president away from the British prime minister and that he had secured his support on major international issues. And who knows whether Stalin was right or not?

The Slippers

All night Major Shaposhnikov of the state security stood at the entrance to Stalin's bedroom, convinced that the leader had decided to spend the night there this time. Shaposhnikov was a huge fellow of about thirty-five, with a round face and broken nose. He was dressed in a dark civilian suit with high shoulder pads and very wide pants, almost like pantaloons, and he was wearing new felt night shoes on his feet.

Shaposhnikov was surprised indeed when he saw Stalin enter the living room from the billiard room in the morning. The leader was wearing pajama bottoms tucked into his socks, and the tunic of the generalissimo of the USSR was unbuttoned. Shaposhnikov noticed that Stalin was unwashed and disheveled, and that the old traces of smallpox appeared as accents on his wrinkled face.

Stalin smiled slyly and said, as he yawned and cleared his throat,

"You've got yourself into a pickle again, Comrade Shaposhnikov. Ah, but you guard your leader poorly. Yesterday as well. Who was on duty the night before last? Potapov? Well, I slept upstairs, and he was guarding the library. No, all is not well in our internal guard.''

Shaposhnikov, standing rigidly before Stalin, decided to raise an objection.

"How can anyone keep up with you, Josif Vissarionovich? The bed is prepared in every room at night, but which one you will choose . . . who knows?''

Stalin scratched his hairy chest, again smiled that sly smile, and said:

"Who knows? To tell you the truth, Shaposhnikov, I myself do not know where I will sleep until the last minute. But *you* must know. It is your duty to know. You are after all an employee of the Ministry of State Security. How does that Russian proverb go? If you want to eat bread, then do not sit on the stove. That is your duty, Comrade Shaposhnikov. And, I might add, a distinguished duty. The Soviet people have entrusted you with the life of Comrade Stalin. The Soviet people are counting on you. Is that not true?''

"Yes, exactly,'' Shaposhnikov answered in clear, military fashion.

"And so, only the Soviet people?''

"The entire progressive world!''

"Sh-sh-sh, not so loud. The question of protecting Comrade Stalin's life is a serious one, you know. I will not deny that I try to deceive, confuse, and trick my bodyguards. And why, allow me to ask you, why?''

"You play with us like a cat with mice,'' Shaposhnikov dared to say.

Stalin became serious. He walked up and down the living room, came up to Shaposhnikov and said:

"No. It is not for amusement, Comrade Shaposhnikov. First of all, I am training you. Second of all, no one, do you hear, no one in the world should know where Comrade Stalin slept, sleeps, or will sleep. There is no greater government secret than that. Do you understand?"

Shaposhnikov began to blink rapidly:

"I understand, Comrade Stalin."

"Very good, very good," the leader said in a milder tone. "Do not fear, I will not tell Comrade Beria. And now . . . good morning, Comrade Shaposhnikov."

Stalin extended his hand. The bodyguard's face lit up with joy. He shook Stalin's hand warmly and said rapturously:

"Good morning, Josif Vissarionovich."

At this moment, Stalin noticed a dish with some eggs on the table.

"Are those eggs fresh?" he asked.

"The housekeeper just brought them in," was the answer.

"That's good, very good. I hope they don't have gunpowder in them."

"I have no way of knowing."

"But you must, you *must,* Comrade Shaposhnikov," said Stalin in a friendly tone.

He then cracked an egg on the table with a swift motion of the hand, drank the contents, and tossed the shell on the plate. He sat in the chair, licked his lips, fixed his mustache and said:

"You were on vacation, weren't you? You are tan. Well, how was it? How's your family?"

Shaposhnikov began to explain with fervor how he had spent his summer vacation on the Black Sea in Sochi, where the Ministry of State Security's sanitorium is situated. He talked about swimming in the sea, about the beach, about playing cards, about wine.

Stalin interrupted:

"Wait a minute, Shaposhnikov, you drank wine . . . or vodka?"

"Vodka," Shaposhnikov noted, slightly embarrassed.

"You are strange people, you Russians," Stalin said. "You drink vodka, but call it wine for some reason."

"It sounds better," Shaposhnikov said, trying to justify himself. "Moreover, wine, like alcohol, has no exact definition."

"Well, go on."

Shaposhnikov changed the subject to his wife, Seraphima, who had gone to Leningrad on business for the first time. Then Shaposhnikov remembered his son, Melor, who had recently left for Artek, the pioneer camp in Crimea, and who planned to go to military school the following year: that is, he wanted to be a gallant Soviet officer, a Stalin officer.

"My boy is smart," said Shaposhnikov. "Every time I go to work, he asks me, 'Papa, will you see Comrade Stalin?' and I answer, 'Yes I will.' 'Oh, papa, what a fortunate person you are, that you will see Comrade Stalin. If I could get only one glance of Stalin, our father, our teacher, our leader, Comrade Stalin.' He said once to me, 'I am ready, papa, to die for Comrade Stalin, because Comrade Stalin protects the interests of workers and peasants.' And once he said, 'I will be a soldier one day, papa, so that I can defend the Soviet land and Comrade Stalin against the enemy.' And another time he said . . ."

"Enough, Comrade Shaposhnikov," Stalin said. "You have a fine son. How did you say he is called?"

"By a new name. This name is born of our new epoch, Comrade Stalin. Melor. M for Marx, E for Engels, L for Lenin, O for October, and R for Revolution."

"Permit me to ask," said Stalin, "where in that case is the S for Stalin?"

"S for Stalin is in my son's heart!" Shaposhnikov shouted, turning red from the strain.

"Ah . . ."

"He loves you so much, Comrade Stalin, so much! He is small but he understands everything as though he had already received a political education."

"And don't they offer enough political education in Soviet schools, Comrade Shaposhnikov?"

"They do, they do," noted Shaposhnikov hurriedly, "but he is special. Melor has already read *A Short Course on the History of the Soviet Communist Party* on his own."

"But that is a little early, I think."

"And of course he hates Americans," continued Shaposhnikov, "Oh, he hates them like fierce animals! He once said, 'You know, papa, I would like to chop Truman's head off.' "

"But that particular head is not worth that much."

"He's little, but he understands," said Shaposhnikov.

An opportunity arose here that the leader almost never passed up: that is, to make fun of a person, to tease him.

"Comrade Shaposhnikov, you are, from what I can gather, sentimental. You are, as the Russian people say, a crybaby. That is interesting. You were once, if I am not mistaken, the Soviet boxing champion. Is that right?"

"That's right."

"What did you do, knock out your opponent and then cry over him?"

Shaposhnikov was clearly embarrassed.

"No, that of course did not happen."

"Someone told me that during the Great Patriotic War you killed Germans with your bare hands. Is that true?"

"Yes, it is."

"But a crybaby."

"My eyes form tears only when I talk about my son, Melor, about how much he loves you, Josif Vissarionovich, about how he considers you his own father."

"Enough, Comrade Shaposhnikov!"

"He's little, but he understands everything," Shaposhnikov said, wiping his eyes.

Stalin was clearly pleased at having made fun of his bodyguard.

"Look here, a partisan, a Communist who answers for the life of Comrade Stalin, a boxer with a broken nose, and a sentimentalist. Very, very interesting. What did you do in your youth, Comrade Shaposhnikov?"

"I, Josif Vissarionovich, at the request of the Lenin Komsomol, worked on the building of a new city, Komsomolsk on the Amur River. I received my first order there. Later, at the request of the Lenin Komsomol, I joined the government organization, that is to say the state security, and I got into the partisans through them."

"How many orders have you received in all?"

"Fourteen."

"Just imagine, fourteen. Almost as many as I have," Stalin again smiled. "And a sentimentalist . . ."

"I am guilty, Comrade Stalin," said Shaposhnikov, with his head lowered.

"And what is that on your feet, Comrade Shaposhnikov?"

"Night shoes . . . my wife brought them from Leningrad . . . as a gift."

"Ah, that's what they are . . . slippers."

"No, Josif Vissarionovich, they are not slippers," Shaposhnikov corrected Stalin, "they are night shoes. Slippers usually have no backs, but these . . ."

"No, Comrade Shaposhnikov, they are *slippers,* slippers," Stalin repeated stubbornly, "and do not argue with me."

"So they are slippers . . ."

"If I say they are slippers, Comrade Shaposhnikov, that means they are slippers. Right?"

"Exactly. They were manufactured by Swiftfoot."

Stalin got up and approached Shaposhnikov.

"Swiftfoot is a well-known factory. It was well known for its quality even before the October Revolution. Interesting. Very interesting. Allow me to look at them closely. Well, take the slippers off your feet."

Shaposhnikov took off the night shoes and handed them to Stalin. The latter began to examine them.

"So, not badly made," he said. "Would you believe, Comrade Shaposhnikov, that I am the son of a shoemaker, an ordinary shoemaker from the Georgian town of Gori? And I know something about shoes."

"The entire progressive world knows that Comrade Stalin is the son of a shoemaker from Gori," Shaposhnikov said.

"I want to congratulate Soviet shoemakers. And how much do these slippers cost?" Stalin asked.

"Truth be known, they were quite expensive. My wife paid forty-six rubles. But if you consider that they are fur-lined . . ."

"You mean to say fur-edged. Yes, that is not cheap. What's so is so. I will take back my congratulations. When your wife can pay ten or twelve rubles for shoes like these, then. . . . A considerate little wife you have, Comrade Shaposhnikov. That's good. Very good. A wife must, absolutely must, show consideration for her husband.''

Stalin returned the shoes to Shaposhnikov, who put them on his feet.

"My wife, Seraphima, is definitely a treasure,'' he said. "Pure gold. When she gave me these night shoes . . .''

"Slippers, slippers!''

". . . she said: 'Wear these in good health, so you will be comfortable when you are on guard, and so there will be no unnecessary noise when you walk up to Comrade Stalin at night to cover him or fix his pillow. Seraphima thinks, of course, that I have such access to you at night.''

"Thank your wife, Comrade Shaposhnikov, for her double consideration, for you and for me. How was it that Seraphima put it: 'So that there will be no unnecessary noise when you walk up to him at night . . .' Interesting. What had your wife in mind, Comrade Shaposhnikov?''

"Felt absorbs noise. That is, in these . . . slippers it is possible to come up to a person and he will not hear you.''

"Will not?''

Stalin's mustache twitched slightly and his right eye suddenly squinted. But Shaposhnikov did not notice this.

"You said, Comrade Shaposhnikov, that it is possible to come up to a person so that he will not even suspect it. Is that not so?''

"That is so,'' Shaposhnikov answered.

"In other words, in these slippers it's possible, in your view, to come up to a person from behind and kill him during his sleep. And, in your view, it's quite easy to do. Right?''

"Yes . . . no . . . I did not have in mind to kill . . ." Confused, Shaposhnikov realized that he had irritated the leader.

"Be quiet, Shaposhnikov," Stalin said abruptly. "Let us perform the following experiment. I will lie down on this sofa and you will walk up to me in your slippers, from that door over there. Carefully, on your tiptoes. And bend over me."

Shaposhnikov waved his hands and asked in a soft voice:

"Why, Josif Vissarionovich?"

"Since when is Comrade Stalin questioned?"

"No, I simply, I . . . I . . ."

"Do as I say."

The leader lay on the sofa, and put his head on the pillow. Shaposhnikov went to the door, tiptoed back to the sofa and bent over Stalin's head.

"Once more, Shaposhnikov!"

The procedure was repeated.

Stalin got up from the sofa and a metallic tone appeared in his voice.

"Do you know, Shaposhnikov, what class struggle means? Do you know, Shaposhnikov, for example, how many anonymous letters are sent to the Kremlin every day, addressed to me? I cannot disclose the exact figure, since that is a government secret, but I will say, enough. More than enough! These people threaten to spit in my face, they threaten to break my nose, and they even threaten to kill me. Yes, yes, kill me. The spitters are few in number, unfortunately, and so are they who wish to break my nose. Primarily, they want to kill, to kill Comrade Stalin."

"Josif Vissarionovich . . ."

"Do not interrupt the leader when he is talking. I remember by heart one of those anonymous letters. 'You, reptile! If I had my way, you whiskered Georgian, I would, starting with your head and ending with your heels, put you through a meat grinder, and without crumbs, just plain. And from your ground meat, fry some meat patties, in lard, and I would feed them to our apartment manager, a member of the Communist party, of course.' How do you like that, Shaposhnikov? Without crumbs even, plain, and not in butter, but in lard . . .''

Shaposhnikov clenched his fists and shouted:

"Shooting someone like that is too good!"

Stalin was pacing up and down the living room and slightly waving his right arm.

"That, you know, is the ABC of class struggle. The Soviet people must be vigilant, vigilant, and once more vigilant. The Soviet people must check everyone—neighbors, comrades, friends, brothers—to make sure that no one is an enemy, an enemy of our socialist society, our people, our Comrade Stalin."

"Correct, correct, Comrade Stalin," Shaposhnikov said decisively, and added carefully, ''but what does this have to do with my night shoes, that is, my slippers?''

"To the point, yes, yes, to the point," Stalin came up close to his bodyguard. "Look me straight in the eye, Shaposhnikov. Do not blink."

Shaposhnikov could not meet Stalin's fixed stare and lowered his eyes. The leader then walked to the Kremlin telephone, picked up the receiver, and dialed four digits.

"Comrade Poskrebyshev?" said Stalin. "It is I. Listen, where is General Vlasek, the head of my bodyguards? Where? In Arkhangelskoe? That's right, I let him off for two weeks. Well, then, call Beria and tell him to come to my *dacha* immediately."

After he hung up, Stalin looked angrily at Shaposhnikov and said:

"And what are you afraid of? An honest man has nothing to fear, Shaposhnikov! The Russian people say: 'A frightened animal runs the farthest.' Ha, ha, ha!"

And directly after this Lieutenant Colonel Litvinenko, the head of internal security at the *dacha,* took Shaposhnikov's pistol away from him and put him under house arrest. The major was locked up in one of the rooms in the *dacha* and watched by the other guards until Marshal Beria's arrival from Moscow.

Beria arrived forty minutes later. Fat, with the neck of a hog, energetic and loud, he was completely bald. The lenses of his pince-nez flashed. He was wearing the uniform of the marshal of the Soviet Union.

When he walked into the living room, Beria saw the housekeeper, a robust, statuesque woman of about thirty, who spotted him, too, and at once turned coquettish. The marshal came up to her so quickly that he almost brushed against her bosom. He almost slapped her on her backside as well, but controlled himself in time, for Stalin was just entering the living room in the full dress of the generalissimo of the USSR with his hair combed and his face cleanly shaven.

The housekeeper immediately left the room.

"Chasing skirts again, Marshal Beria?"

"Good day, Josif Vissarionovich, batono," said Beria, with an embarrassed smile.

They started to speak in Georgian.

"I have heard that you pay your mistresses 500 rubles for a session."

"What are you saying, Josif Vissarionovich? That is only gossip. Who told you?"

"It is unimportant who, the important thing is that it is true. Well, first of all 500 rubles is too much. Secondly, I would like to know whether you pay this out of your own pocket or whether you charge it to the Ministry of Internal Affairs? Assigning it to—how should I put it—operating costs?"

"Josif Vissarionovich, I swear to you by my honor that that is not true. Only an intrigue. From my enemy. It must be Malenkov."

"Malenkov or not," Stalin said, "you, Comrade Beria, hold an important position in the Soviet government, and the Soviet government, you must understand, is not a stud farm. I am afraid that I may have to have you castrated."

"Comrade Stalin!"

"Who sent this fat-assed woman here, this new house-keeper?"

"She is from the first directorate of my ministry."

"So you sent her here."

"General Vlasek is fully in charge of the first directorate, Josif Vissarionovich, batono. I swear by my honor I don't know her. I saw her today for the first time."

"Good. Take her with you into your organization. Let her serve you. Now sit down right here. This is an important matter."

Beria sat in the chair across from Stalin. The leader lit a cigarette, but did not offer one to Beria. Beria did not smoke. Then Stalin said:

"Do you remember, marshal, when that Fascist scoundrel, Hitler's minister, Ribbentrop, used to visit us, before the war, do you remember how I introduced you to him?"

"I remember."

"How?"

"You pointed at me and said, 'This is our gestapo.' "

Stalin smiled. He liked it that Beria always guessed his thoughts and was often right on target.

"True, true, Comrade Beria. Well then, if you are really our gestapo, you must know everything. *Absolutely everything.*"

"I try, batono, Josif Vissarionovich."

"Stop calling me by this Georgian batono," Stalin burst out. "What kind of batono am I? I am Stalin. Is that clear?"

"Forgive me, Comrade Stalin. I was joking."

"I am not up to your jokes," Stalin said. "I don't have time for them. I have, as you know, serious business to attend to. So . . . if you are our gestapo, please solve the following problem."

Stalin took Shaposhnikov's night shoes from the cupboard and dangled them under Beria's nose.

"What is this?"

"Night shoes, if I am not mistaken," Beria answered.

"No, you are mistaken, Comrade Beria, as usual. These are not night shoes, but slippers. Do you understand, slippers?" Stalin put the shoes on the round table next to the chairs.

Beria agreed at once. "I did not examine them as carefully as I should have. They are slippers."

"Felt."

"Yes, yes, felt."

"And to whom do they belong, Comrade Beria?"

"Mm . . ."

"Mm. All you can do is moo. Our gestapo!"

"Lord in heaven, I don't know!"

"All right, I will tell you to whom these slippers belong. They belong to one of my bodyguards, Major Shaposhnikov. Is that name familiar to you?"

Beria livened up.

"But, of course, I know him. Shaposhnikov, the giant. A former boxing champion. And where is he?"

"He is under house arrest. His weapons confiscated."

"His weapons confiscated?" Beria grew pale. "What happened, Josif Vissarionovich?"

"Luckily, nothing has happened so far," Stalin said, "but it could have happened. And if it had happened . . . There is a suggestion that this Shaposhnikov was going to sneak up to me at night in those slippers and kill me." Stalin's cheekbones became pronounced and a devilish glow appeared in his eyes. "Whose idea was *that*, Comrade Beria?" he demanded.

"To kill you? Shaposhnikov? No, that is not possible." Beria said this involuntarily, although he immediately realized that he had to agree with the leader's suspicions.

Stalin slammed his fist on the table, which he very rarely did.

"I am asking you, marshal, whose idea was that? It is your responsibility to know whose idea. Or perhaps it was your idea, Comrade Beria?"

"How can you think that, Josif Vissarionovich, how can you, batono . . . ?"

"Again, batono?" Stalin shouted angrily.

"Forgive me, please forgive me." Beria got up from his chair and almost fell on his knees, bent over as though he were expecting the final blow.

But then Stalin said calmly:

"Who does Shaposhnikov work for? The British or the Americans?"

Like a drowning man clutching for a straw, Beria said:

"The British. That is so, Comrade Stalin. I suspected this."

Stalin became almost cheerful.

"That's what I thought. Churchill. My old friend, Winnie. Although he is no longer in power." And then in a businesslike manner he added: "Hold an investigation immediately, Beria. Get a full confession from Shaposhnikov and report back to me."

Stalin left the living room. Beria took Shaposhnikov's night shoes from the table, turned them around in his hands, raised them over his head, and examined them from all sides.

"Went crazy again, the Georgian turkey," he murmured.

With the night shoes in his hands, Beria walked over to the room where Shaposhnikov was being held under house arrest. The major looked drawn. He had lost perhaps ten kilograms in the past hour. His face was ashen. He blinked often, which clearly reflected the fear he felt. He sat shriveled up in a chair, but when Beria came in, he jumped up, his arms in line with the seams of his trousers.

"Shaposhnikov, are these your night shoes?" Beria asked.

"They are mine."

"Where did you get them?"

"Well, my wife brought them from Leningrad . . . Swiftfoot . . . as a present."

"Ass."

"What?"

"You're an ass, that's what. Now you will answer with your head."

"But for what? Comrade Beria, I didn't do anything."

"Eh, what can I do with you?" Beria said. "Don't you know, you blockhead, that our leader is obsessed with class enemies. He sees them everywhere. Why did you give him the opportunity, you overgrown dunderhead. He's a psychopath, understand?''

Blinking even more frequently, Shaposhnikov said: ''What are you saying, Comrade Beria? Who are you talking about? Comrade Stalin?''

''You idiot,'' Beria said, ''I am talking to you honestly, because you are already a dead man, a corpse.''

''Comrade Beria . . .''

''Sit and answer my questions!'' ordered Beria as he sat down himself. ''Where were you born? In the country?''

''In the country. In Altai.''

''Is your father alive?''

''No. He died a long time ago.''

''That's good. What was he? A rich peasant?''

''No, no, a poor one. And he had a big family.''

''Were you ever abroad?''

''In Germany, of course. During the war.''

''And after the war?''

''For a short time in Berlin.''

''That's good, that you were in Berlin. That's sufficient evidence, because there were British in Berlin, too.''

''What?''

''You will have to write a confession now. The leader of all peoples of the world needs your confession. Here is paper and a pen. Now write.''

''Why a confession? About what?'' asked Shaposhnikov.

''This is not for you to think about. Write exactly what I dictate, as follows: To the Minister of Internal Affairs of the USSR, Marshal Beria, Lavrenti Pavlovich. From Major Shaposhnikov, and your initials. 'I confess that after the period of collectivization of farmers, when my father was dispossessed as a kulak in Altai and sent to a concentration camp, I bore a grudge against Soviet power and swore to revenge myself on account of my dear father.' "

Shaposhnikov jumped up from his chair.

"Lavrenti Pavlovich, what is all this?"

Beria said evenly, "If you want to live, write what I dictate. If you refuse, I will call Bakhcho Kobulov and you know what will happen then.

"But for what? For what?"

"After you finish writing, you will understand." Beria lowered his voice to a whisper. "We will wrap the old man around our fingers . . ." His voice returned to normal and he continued to dictate Shaposhnikov's confession. " 'When I was in Berlin, I, Shaposhnikov, came in contact with a representative of the British intelligence service. I received the code name Shakespeare, and later made my way into the first directorate of the state security as Stalin's bodyguard. My mission, in accordance with instructions from the British Colonel Cook, no, Smith, which I received through the British embassy in Moscow, was to kill Stalin at night, when he was asleep.' That's it. Short and to the point. Nothing more is needed. Now sign."

"Comrade Beria, that's not true! Not true!" Shaposhnikov screamed.

"Shut your mouth, blockhead! Did I say it was true? Of course it is not true, but it is essential for our great father and leader. He will make this untruth into a major ideological and class truth. He is a splendid manipulator in this area, a real juggler."

"I love Stalin, like my other father! Comrade Stalin is the dearest person to me in the whole world." Shaposhnikov was choking with sobs.

"Don't pull my leg. Sign this confession and I will send

you to one of the Soviet republics. To Kazakhstan maybe, or, if you want, to the Far East regional division of our ministry. I have one of my men in Khabarovsk, General Gvishiani, also Georgian. Stalin won't know anything about it. I will tell him that I had you shot. Your salary will have to be lowered. You will take your family with you. Understand that this is the only way out. The leader of the progressive world needs you to be a British spy and terrorist. Once he's decided this, the matter is closed. You cannot change his mind. He is as stubborn as a Caucasian mule. Moreover, you are tall, Shaposhnikov, and our leader does not like tall people. In a word, sign the confession, and go to see Kobulov. He will find you a suitable position.''

"Lavrenti Pavlovich," Shaposhnikov was in despair, "there is no evidence that I was a British terrorist.''

"The night shoes?''

Now Shaposhnikov genuinely cried. He sobbed, wiped his tears, blew his nose, jerked his shoulders.

"Idiot, what are you crying for? Do you think tears will help?''

"Lavrenti Pavlovich, I have a wife, a son, I have been in the party since 1938. I have served the Soviet state faithfully and honestly all my life.''

"Ha! There were more important ones than you who also served the Soviet state.''

"I believe in Comrade Stalin completely!''

"If you believe in him completely, then what is all this talk about? He said that you are a British agent. That is all.''

"I am ready to die for Comrade Stalin!'' Shaposhnikov declared.

"Here is your chance,'' Beria said with a laugh. ''Eh, Shaposhnikov, stop babbling. Everyone is sick of these words. If you want me to save your life under the circumstances I proposed to you, sign the confession. And don't delay.''

''But how can I?''

''Be a man! You have become a wet rag. You must see this as a joke. The old man cannot live without these jokes. He gets bored. But I promise you that we will outsmart him, and we *will* outsmart him.''

''Lavrenti Pavlovich, you won't betray me?''

''What are you saying,'' Beria said in a disgusted tone, ''don't you trust Beria? When have I ever betrayed my fellow workers? My people worship me. I will never wrong them.''

Shaposhnikov signed the confession. Afterward he said:

''Long live great Stalin!''

''Long live great Stalin,'' Beria echoed.

When the marshal returned to the living room, he telephoned his deputy, Kobulov, and said:

''Listen Bakhcho, Major Shaposhnikov of the leader's bodyguards will come to you for a new assignment. But do not give him anything. It has become apparent that he is an agent of Churchill's. What? Stalin himself made it apparent. Yes. This Shaposhnikov must be liquidated immediately. Yes, straight to Lubyanka.''

Beria had just hung up when Stalin entered the living room.

''Well? How is Shaposhnikov?'' he asked.

''He confessed to everything, Josif Vissarionovich,'' Beria answered. ''He had already established contact with the British intelligence in Berlin.''

The marshal handed Shaposhnikov's confession to the leader. Stalin skimmed it, grinned and said:

"You are a rascal, Comrade Beria."

"What did you say, Josif Vissarionovich?"

"Is it permissible to ask what you did with Shaposhni-kov? Did you get rid of him?"

"Not yet," Beria said sarcastically. "Would you like to pardon him?"

"Let him be on your conscience, Beria," said Stalin. "There is no mercy for enemies. Only one thing. He has a son, a wonderful little boy called Melor. Make arrange-ments for him next year at the military school. He will make a dashing Soviet officer. I would even say, a Stalin officer. In the Soviet society, Comrade Beria, a son does not have to answer for his father's sins, you know. And Shaposhni-kov's wife, Seraphima, should be sent outside Moscow's limits, but she should be given a job. Let her live and work. We Communists are not avengers. Isn't that so, Comrade Beria?"

"Exactly so, Comrade Stalin."

"As far as these slippers are concerned, it must be noted that our Soviet shoemakers do not work haphazardly any-more, and I suggest that they be sent to the Museum of the Revolution."

"Who? Soviet shoemakers?"

"The slippers, the slippers, you fool. It would not be a bad idea if they were preserved there on exhibit to show methods used in plots by imperialist secret services and ter-rorist centers. Let it be a lesson to posterity. For history, Comrade Beria. It was a trick of Winston Churchill's. Send him a telegram and inform him that his agent, Shakespeare, has fallen. Has slipped on his own slippers. And now you can return to Moscow, Comrade Beria. I do not need you any longer. Although, wait a minute. Come here."

Beria approached the leader, who, with the gesture of a magician, took something "from the air" and fastened that something to Beria's chest.

"This is a bonus," Stalin said grinning. "Tell Comrade Gorkin to make this official by a decree of the Presidium of the Supreme Soviet. Allow me to congratulate you, Hero of Socialist Labor. I congratulate you with a gold star."

Before he left Stalin's *dacha* for Moscow, Beria again saw the buxom housekeeper. This time he did not restrain himself and pinched her on her backside.

"Ah, marshal," she cried out flirtatiously.

That evening, at his own home on Little Nikitski Lane, with his wife, Nina, and son, Sergo, Beria celebrated his new title of Hero of Socialist Labor.

The Big Life

One thing I can say for certain, the most important job we Soviet deputy ministers had was guarding the rotator—the Kremlin telephone—around the clock, in case Stalin called. He, of course, almost never called; however, the chief of his secretariat did. We referred to him as Comrade Stalin's helper. He was a man of bony build and gloomy expression whose name was Poskrebyshev (he had replaced Mekhlis). His call was considered Stalin's call. We sat by the rotator, or, to be more exact, *on* the rotator from 11 to 6 during the day, and from 10 to 3 at night. The minister of cinematography, a red-haired man with a turned-up nose who resembled the last czar of Russia, Nikolas II, even rose from his chair when he talked to Poskrebyshev. Moreover, there was a rotator on the tennis court where our minister spent his Sundays, so that Poskrebyshev could reach him at any time.

With regard to the night vigils, our second deputy minister of cinematography (I was the *first* deputy minister), Oleg Shcherpinsky, would cry out after his lavish, government-subsidized dinner:

"If the leader doesn't sleep, the whole country does not sleep."

When our minister left for vacation at a top-level sanitorium located between Gagra and Sukhumi on the Black Sea, I took his place at the rotator. In a day or two it rang, with particular ceremony I thought. I almost flinched, but immediately picked up the receiver and identified myself. A dry and commanding voice said:

"This is Poskrebyshev. Bring the film *The Big Life* to the Kremlin tonight. The viewing time is exactly midnight."

At that moment, in all honesty, I felt that there were forces beyond my control. My brain decided for me and my muscles submitted. I rose from my chair exactly as the minister did.

Oh yes, Poskrebyshev was quite a person, I would say. If he ordered *The Big Life* to be sent to the Kremlin at night, that meant that Stalin himself would watch it.

All further action was carried out automatically through special channels: that is, through the division of screening and through a special sector of the state security in our ministry to which entry was prohibited, even to the minister. The film was sent to the Kremlin. Due to the absence of the minister, however, I was obliged to sit at the control panel in the viewing room.

A few words about Stalin and cinematography. The leader loved movies, and not just because Lenin considered film "the most important of the arts," but simply in human terms. Stalin suffered from insomnia, and would order two full-length films to be sent to him for one night. These were, as a rule, not our Soviet films but American ones requisitioned in Germany right after the war and carried off to Moscow. For the most part, the films were westerns, with cowboys, shoot-outs, bandits, sheriffs, and so on.

It was not easy for the minister to show a new Soviet movie. Without Stalin's permission, he did not have the right to release a film. I know, for example, that viewing of the movie *The Battle of Stalingrad* was delayed for almost a month. Every time that Poskrebyshev called the minister and ordered him to send two cowboy films to the Kremlin, the minister tactfully advised Poskrebyshev to show Stalin *The Battle of Stalingrad,* then a film with a shoot-out with American handguns.

As he sat at the control panel, our minister would translate the dialogue in the Hollywood films. What's more, he didn't know English—not one word. The question arises, how did he cope with this problem? This is how: Before the showing, the minister would view the film several times with our professional interpreters. They worked out a translation for him. He would then lock himself in his study, cancel all his meetings, and learn that translation by heart. At night he would set off for the Kremlin or to Stalin's *dacha* at Kuntsevo.

It should be added that our minister never made a mistake in the translation. He was particularly gifted in this respect. He once informed me proudly that Stalin himself would give the cues in advance, once he'd seen his favorite movies five or six times.

The Big Life, a monumental film, was created by one of the best Soviet film producers, the late Leonid Lukov—a very nice fellow, kind-hearted, sociable, a great conversationalist, and a lady's man. They don't speak badly of the dead, do they? Well then, I say he was a very nice fellow.

The film was about the contemporary Donbas, the richest coal basin in the USSR, about its people and how they rebuilt the key region of the nation destroyed by the Germans during the war. The movie was well-made. With substance. Without fear. The producer made his mark, so to speak, through the realism. I personally liked the movie. And most of the ministry people reacted to it in a positive way.

The minister himself was a tough customer. Let's say he never jumped into the fire before it was necessary. He did not express his opinion, although after viewing *The Big Life,* when I asked him "Well?," he answered, "A little gloomy." He was waiting.

Poskrebyshev had been informed of *The Big Life,* but he had called for westerns to be sent. In order to speed up matters, the minister had succeeded in stealing Andrei Zhdanov into our ministry. Until that time Zhdanov had not viewed films on our premises. He was then the secretary of the Central Commitee of the Soviet Communist party on ideological questions, including art and literature. We were all aware that Zhdanov was close to Stalin and that he sometimes played Beethoven on the piano for him.

Zhdanov liked *The Big Life*. He praised the film. Leonid Lukov strutted around like a peacock. The minister was heartened, counting on the fact that the leader would react positively to the film. Zhdanov's opinion seemed to be a good omen. Poskrebyshev, however, continued to order westerns and *The Big Life* continued to lie in the metal boxes.

Summer vacation had approached. Even though our minister loved to give awards, titles, and decorations, he went off to the Black Sea. I was to call the sanitorium if anything important came up. After my phone conversation with Poskrebyshev, I immediately got in touch with the minister and told him that Stalin would finally view *The Big Life.* The minister became nervous and wanted to fly to Moscow, but then he changed his mind and ordered me to call him at the sanitorium the following morning.

"Make a preliminary list of candidates for awards and decorations," he said, "and don't forget me and you. Throw in an outline of the film for submission for the Stalin Prize."

I can assure you that he dove into the sea with particular enjoyment that day, and won a tennis match either with the minister of shipbuilding or with the minister of textile manufacturing.

Meanwhile, at 11:30 at night I "flew" to the leader in the minister's personal car with the governmental "cuckoo" horn, which magically stopped all traffic. Oh, what an exciting feeling! You go nonstop along Gorki Street, through Manezhnaya Square to the Borovitsky Gate at the Kremlin.

I had had occasion to see Stalin at parades, at party congresses and conferences. But I had not seen him up close and had never spoken with him. I must confess I was as nervous as a youth right before a first date.

The viewing started late. About quarter past one. I was sitting before the control panel when the door of the viewing room opened and Stalin came in, followed by a fat general with a true peasant face. This was probably Vlasek, the head of Stalin's bodyguards. After them came Beria and Malenkov, the most influential members of the Politburo, talking softly as though they were at a funeral. Then the rest of the Politburo filed in in silence, about ten or twelve of them. Stalin glanced in my direction and walked over to the first row. He occupied the seat to the right. Vlasek sat in the same row, on the opposite side. Beria and Malenkov sat on the left of Stalin in the second row. Molotov, Voroshilov, Kaganovich, Zhdanov and other comrades and disciples distributed themselves over the third and fourth rows. This was done in such a way that one could picture their last names on the back of each chair. Several characters from the Kremlin guards entered the room as well.

Stalin was dressed in his generalissimo tunic with the top button unbuttoned. He looked exactly as I had seen him in film chronicles. Pockmarked, short, I would even say puny, with very quick and stealthy eyes. He put his hand on the empty chair next to him and looked toward Beria and Malenkov, who at once turned in Stalin's direction like roosters. I noticed that Stalin again glanced at me and asked Beria something. Beria then glanced at me and probably explained to Stalin that I was replacing the minister of cinematography, who had gone on vacation to the Black Sea.

A minute passed, then two. I was awaiting a command. At last the leader nodded. In a loud, commanding voice Beria said:

"Let us begin, comrades."

I pressed the button. *The Big Life* began.

Here, two or three meters from me, was the brain of our party, the genius of all mankind whose name was known throughout the world. I saw his head, his shoulder. It seemed to me that I heard the tops of his boots (into which his military striped pants were tucked) squeak.

My mind was flooded with emotion. Why did I feel deep respect, but also something completely contradictory, a certain vexation? Was it because Stalin's comrades and disciples moved like automatons, like tin soldiers? Why was I vexed? In any group of people, there are always dependent human mechanisms. It seems to me *now* that I felt vexation *then,* but *then,* to be honest, I was a tin soldier myself.

Stalin coughed. He wasn't smoking cigarettes, for some

reason, but a pipe, which I had been told he did rarely. I could see streams of smoke in the rays of the movie projector. In a break in the dialogue, Stalin said:

"It's too loud. Turn it down a bit."

I turned the knob on the control panel to the left; I could sense a light note of dissatisfaction in Stalin's voice. In the middle of the movie he got up and walked around the viewing room. Then he sat down again and shrugged his shoulders as though squirming. I had the feeling that everyone had stopped breathing.

Suddenly Beria's voice boomed out:

"This is a disgrace! The devil only knows! We gave millions of rubles for the restoration of the Donbas, and they show us half-ruined settlements, dead mines, hungry and dirty people, a life to make you think that the Soviet Army freed the Donbas from German occupation only yesterday."

My blood ran cold. I never expected Beria to venture his opinion first, especially without seeing the entire film. I wondered why Stalin didn't interrupt him by saying something like, "Be quiet, Comrade Beria! I haven't asked for your opinion yet," or "Go away! Don't disturb me while I'm watching a movie."

Stalin got up again, turned his back to the screen and said:

"You are right, Comrade Beria. Either we are throwing money away where nothing is being done, or the director of this movie, if you can call it that, is trying to keep up with cheap everyday realism and has lost sight of party instinct."

These words of the leader were sufficient. Voices expressing disgust resounded from all sides. Stalin's comrades demolished *The Big Life* in unison, so to speak.

As I listened to them, I could imagine Leonid Lukov's face, deathly pale.

Stalin scratched his right mustache, then raised his hand and everyone was silent. He addressed me directly.

"Comrade from the Ministry of Cinematography (he did not call me deputy minister), turn down the volume. Nobody needs that idiotic noise from the screen."

I turned the knob as far as possible.

"Now, I have a question to ask you: Tell me please, did anyone from the Central Committee see this picture before we did?"

Alas, human behavior is far from being understood. I say this now looking back on that night and trying to analyze myself. Man is at times not in control of himself. I am a Marxist-Leninist. But what should we expect from other ordinary mortals? There are forces outside us, and they are often in control. It was such an unknown force, perhaps it could be called life force, that made me say without thinking, "No, nobody saw it before you, Comrade Stalin."

Andrei Zhdanov did not contradict me. He did not say that I had lied. He said nothing. That was how dependent and worthless the position of the ideological boss was. He hid from the leader the fact that he had seen the film. That tin soldier who sometimes played Beethoven for Stalin.

"Very good," said the leader, "in that case an appropriate document should be published in *Pravda*. A resolution should be made in the Central Committee, Comrade Zhdanov. Policy conclusions will of course be needed. A movie in which our Soviet life is blackened is not acceptable. We don't need these ragged men on the screen, they aren't the real builders of communism!"

"The devil only knows, Josif Vissarionovich!" Beria cried.

"The devil only knows, Lavrenti Pavlovich!" Stalin echoed. "The workers for our patriotic Soviet cinematography must understand that socialist realism, since the time of Maxim Gorky, teaches an artist to look ahead to determine the leading tendencies of the time and of the epoch, and not to follow petty bourgeois aesthetic devices. All that neorealism and other nonsense."

"Nonsense, Josif Vissarionovich," Beria said.

And Malenkov joined in. "Exactly so, Josif Vissarionovich."

The leader spoke softly with his strong Georgian accent, pausing at random as usual, for he knew that no one dared to correct or interrupt him.

I was thinking of heads at that moment. Of human heads. Here, before the screen with *The Big Life* still flashing on it, Stalin and his disciples were beginning to chop off the heads of those who had made this film. Whose head would be chopped off first? Lukov's? The minister's? Mine?

"Comrade Zhdanov, make sure, if you please, that the Central Committee's resolution will be studied at party meetings and not only among film makers. This document should be central. Art and literature must educate our masses in the communistic spirit. That is the basic problem. Is that right?"

There was a loud chorus of "rights." Beria was particularly active. But Malenkov did not lag behind. That eunuch-like man with elephant legs who a few years before had been only first secretary of the Baumanski District Committee of the Communist party in Moscow. I think he had been promoted because of his ability to write speeches. And Stalin personally valued his ability to write speeches, to make resolutions, and so forth.

Then the leader left, escorted by General Vlasek and

some of his bodyguards. The film continued while comrades and disciples proceeded to run *The Big Life* into the ground. The hatchet job went on in the dark for a long time. Beria finally barked:

"Stop this ridiculous film!"

I pressed the button. The film stopped. The lights were turned on.

Later I walked home rather than taking the minister's car. At the corner of the empty Arbat Street, boys in caps (agents of the state security) were guarding Stalin's route. That meant that the leader had not yet left for his *dacha*, but was still at the Kremlin. Special trucks equipped with water tanks were hosing the asphalt. I walked slowly, having taken off my hat. A driver hustling for extra money stopped a government-owned Pobeda and asked me if I wanted a ride. I said no.

Moscow at dawn is particularly attractive. I don't know why. There is something about it. Perhaps it is even poetic. Perhaps our Soviet poet Mayakovski walked at night along the empty streets of Moscow, creating his epochal, sharp verses in time to his footsteps. I had been interested in Mayakovski when I was in the Komsomol.

What was I deliberating? What was in my heart? Of course, I deliberated about the heads. Perhaps tonight or to-morrow night someone from the secret police would come for me and I would disappear without a trace. I remembered countless victims: friends, comrades, colleagues. Actually, I had nothing to lose. My wife had a job in food manufac-turing, my son was a university student. Most probably, they would not be touched; I was not a counterrevolu-tionary.

Fear, however, was not my main emotion at the time. I

felt deep guilt, our collective guilt, the guilt of the cinema-
tographers and all the workers in our patriotic Soviet cinematography, as Comrade Stalin had said. As I crossed the
Smolenski Bridge, I repeated aloud what Molotov had said:
"You outsmarted yourselves." Yes, we had outsmarted
ourselves. We had not seen the same things in the film as
Stalin had. We had turned out to be the Philistines.

I could not then imagine that the leader could be wrong. I
knew that it was I who was wrong. I even began to prepare a
letter of explanation to the Central Committee about myself.
I would, of course, repent for this major error.

It had been established that way.

Another thought troubled me. How had Beria decided to
make such a bold move? Apparently, he had studied the
leader so carefully that any slight gesture became more sig-
nificant for him than for the rest of us. Perhaps Beria had
risked speaking out because Stalin had said, "turn it down a
bit," perhaps because he smoked a pipe and not a cigarette.
Or because he put his left hand on the chair—his left, not
his right—or because he moved his shoulders.

When I got home, I had some tea without sugar, and lay
on the couch fully clothed. It wasn't worth it to wake up my
wife in the bedroom. I couldn't sleep. I kept listening. The
window of my study opened out on the courtyard. In fact,
cars stopped in our courtyard several times. I thought to
myself: "And what if they are after me?" The leader could
have given General Vlasek orders after he left the viewing
room. He had called me "the comrade from the ministry"
for some reason. I had not translated cowboy movies for
him. Yes, Stalin could have ordered the general to do anything. He was wise, Stalin. He kept this Vlasek at his side
constantly.

It had been established that way.

The next morning at ten, I arrived at the ministry and saw Leonid Lukov there. He looked thinner, his face was very pale. He held a letter addressed to the Central Committee, admitting to all of his mistakes and asking the Central Committee to allow him to keep his party card. Lukov had somehow gotten wind of what had happened the night before at the Kremlin. I left him in the reception room and made a call to the minister.

"Hello. Well, then, will we be drinking champagne?" the minister asked joyfully.

"You, Comrade Minister," I said, "must fly to Moscow right away. Heads are going to roll. A conductor for the orchestra is absolutely necessary. Which head to put first, which second, and so on. You can do that, I can't."

I told the minister all that had happened. He paused dramatically and said:

"No, you resolve everything yourself. I am on vacation. I would rather stay here and play tennis."

And he hung up. He had decided to wash his hands of the matter and put the burden on my shoulders. However, that was not how it turned out. The next day the minister was summoned to the capital by a telegram from Zhdanov. He came immediately. He took the place of conductor and started wielding the baton. During the following week, the historic resolution of the Central Committee of the Soviet Communist party on the subject of the movie *The Big Life* was issued. It appeared on the front page of *Pravda*.

Yes, heads did roll. There were renunciations, repentances, critical articles by the dozen.

In conclusion, I will mention only one detail. At noon the day after the showing, that memorable noon, the rotator began to vibrate. I was startled and answered the phone by identifying myself. Beria was calling me. This is what he said:

"Good day, Comrade Deputy Minister. You are a fine fellow. You lied beautifully last night. Do you think that the leader did not know that Zhdanov had seen the movie before we did?" He laughed cynically and added, "You did the right thing. I congratulate you. There was no choice in the matter. You had to lie. And Comrade Stalin appreciated that."

I remained silent. Did I feel any remorse? The devil only knows. Probably not.

Batya, Make Me a General!

Vasily, wearing a military uniform with the rank of Air Force colonel, entered the living room. When he saw his father, he paused beside a large chair and leaned against it in such a way that Stalin would not notice that he was drunk. However, his dry lips, the protruding veins on his temples, and his sweaty forehead gave him away.

Stalin's son from his second marriage was of medium height, thin, with red hair and freckles; his face was Russian, but his profile was Georgian, a copy of his father's. He moved confidently, like a soldier, but he spoke Russian like a Moscow taxi driver, in a jerky and sloppy way, throwing in both decent and indecent words.

Vasily coughed, trying to get his father's attention.

Stalin, wearing the uniform of the generalissimo of the USSR and newly polished boots, was sitting on the couch, reading a manuscript without glasses. He was clearly in no hurry to acknowledge his son, even though the night before he had appointed this hour for a meeting at Blizhnaya, the *dacha*.

71

"Batya, father," Vasily said.

Stalin raised his eyes and squinted.

"Drunk again?"

Vasily shrugged his shoulders, as though he had not understood.

"What are you talking about?"

"Oh, kind people," Stalin said with an ironic smile, "look at the son I have. Scum. You drank a lot this time?"

"Just a drop, I swear in the name of the party," and Vasily hiccuped, something he did only after drinking a liter of vodka.

"Can't you do without that? Especially when you have a meeting with your father?" asked Stalin. "The Russians have a saying: 'A drop—one sip for a sparrow, but it hollows a stone.' Have you heard this?"

"Yes, I have heard it. And that's right."

"What's right?"

"Exactly. I am hollowed stone. But you, batya, are granite. Listen old man, make me a general."

"No."

"Papasha, please!"

"I would rather demote you to the ranks again. I will make you a lieutenant—no, a sergeant—in our great armed forces."

"E-e-e-e, you're winding up your organ again. Go to hell! You've demoted me a hundred times. 'Our great armed forces.' You genius, with your morals, you had no right having children. You are like Ivan the Terrible. You torture."

"I, torture?"

"You torture."

Stalin burst out laughing and returned to his manuscript.

He had that ability to ignore people who were at the same table or in the same room with him. And he would do this suddenly, as though he cut you off with a knife.

"May I smoke?" Vasily asked.

Stalin did not answer. Vasily took a pack of Kazbek from his pocket and lighted a cigarette, depositing the used match in an ashtray. He inhaled, which made his heart lighter, and he hiccuped again, and said:

"Batya, make me a general."

"No," said Stalin, his attention still on the manuscript.

"Please." Vasily was almost childlike.

"No."

"Papasha!"

Stalin laid his manuscript aside.

"Papasha sounds like a character in a musical comedy, Vas'ka. And does Comrade Stalin resemble a musical comedy papasha? Respectful sons do not address their fathers in that way."

"What about Vas'ka," shouted Vasily. "Do respectful fathers address their sons that way? In the great writer Maxim Gorky's plays there are all kinds of 'Nas'kas' and 'Vas'kas'."

Stalin was momentarily taken aback by his son's on-slaught, but as always under such circumstances, he squinted and deflected the conversation.

"Who said Gorky is a great Russian writer?"

Vasily did not back off:

"Listen, don't make a fool of me. Gorky used to come over for dinner. And if he were not great, you would not have invited him. Malicious tongues have it that you had him sent back to his great-grandfathers. Perhaps you had a difference of opinion."

Stalin's voice became metallic, the voice Vasily feared. "Repeat what you said."

"That was not I, it was malicious tongues," Vasily said. "You know, batya, that I am not involved in politics. Kill anyone you want. You're Stalin. Not I."

Stalin sighed.

"Vasilek, you have never been the best in our family. It seems suitable to quote a Russian proverb: 'In every good head of cabbage, there is fungus.' Is that not true, Comrade Colonel?"

Knowing that it would displease his father, Vasily shouted as loud as he could in military fashion:

"Exactly so, Comrade Generalissimo of the Soviet Union!"

"Sh-sh-sh." Stalin screwed up his face. "Don't yell, you ass."

"Batya, may I sit down?" Vasily spoke quietly but sarcastically. "Even asses like to sit."

"All right, sit down, you menace."

"What exactly are you reading?"

Stalin, warming a bit, took up the manuscript and thumbed through it.

"It's a film script. About me. Another one. Listen to what intelligent people write about your father. Listen and wind it on your whiskers."

Stalin stopped riffling through the manuscript and read the following: "In the never-ending fields of Russia, Stalin appeared . . ."

"Baloney!" Vasily interrupted. "They should have written: 'In the never-ending fields of Russia, our dear teacher, the great Stalin appeared.' "

"Crawling before your own father?" Stalin laughed.

"I have no choice, old man."

Stalin got up from the couch, walked about the living room and said good naturedly:

"But I still will not make you a general, my son. Even though I know you dream of it at night."

Vasily sprawled on the chair and tried to convince his father of his rightness, gesticulating vaguely and hiccuping twice.

"Try to understand, old man, put yourself in my position. What am I? A colonel? A colonel. And who am I surrounded by? Generals. They break their backs before me, and are ready to kiss my ass. Why? Because I am Stalin's son. Understand?"

"Who wouldn't." Stalin put his hands behind his back and continued to walk about the living room. "But don't you think, Vasilek, that our great armed forces have bred generals as though they were chickens? Wherever you look, there is a general. As the Russian people say: 'Seven generals to one corporal.' "

"I don't care about them," Vasily said. "Count the number of generals you have, the number of corporals, and the number of privates. Promote me, and cut down the number of generals, arrest them, hang them, shoot them, do what you want. You're Stalin. Not me!"

Stalin stopped pacing and looked at his son.

"What can I say, its's logical, Vasily."

"Well, then." Vasily breathed more easily.

"Only one question, Vasily Josifovich: Do you deserve the title of general?"

Vasily became angry.

"E-e-e-e, here we go again, the same thing. Vasily Josifovich. Addressing me formally. Don't try to imitate Ivan the Terrible, batya. He, too, they say, addressed his son formally. You ask whether I deserve the title of general? Of course I do. Just as one needs water. One hundred percent. Who fought against Hitler? Who was a fighter pilot? And I'm not just doodling when I say that, you know.''

Stalin suddenly asked:

"Is is true that you have your own football team? By that I mean the Air Force football team. Don't they just call it 'Vasya Stalin's team.' Is that right or isn't it?''

"Well, let's assume that it is . . .''

"I heard,'' Stalin continued, "that you act like a czar. You entice players from other teams, for example, Dynamo. Are you aspiring to the Winner's Cup of the Soviet Union? Yes or no?''

"So what?'' Vasily hiccuped.

"I have heard that your team has its own airplane. All this while you are still a colonel. What will happen when you are a general? The Queen of England is a patron of swans, and the Son of Stalin—of football players.''

"Beria probably told you these things. What a blabbermouth that head of the secret police is. He spies on me. What a life! Even Stalin's son has no peace and quiet from the state security. Beria should tell you about his mistresses instead.''

"I know about his mistresses. You yourself don't live without them.''

"Me?''

"You.''

"Well, I am a man . . .''

"You have quite a turnover of women. First it was a swimmer, then a skater, and now it's a discus thrower. You are practicing in the world of sports.''

"So Beria blabbed about that, too. What a race of people you are, you Georgians! Gossips, troublemakers, plotters, spies—and murderers of course."

"Aren't you Georgian?"

"I am Russian. My mother . . ."

"Don't mention your mother, you scum!"

"And why not?" Vasily asked. "Mama would have been glad if I were promoted to general."

Stalin crossed to the window and stood there for a long time. Then he turned to his son and said in a lowered voice:

"Your mother, Vasily, was an angel."

"And who sent her to her grave?" Vasily burst out. "You."

"Shut up, you no-good!" Stalin shouted.

Vasily remained firm. "Don't make so much noise, batya. I know you well. We have not met for the first time. You are cruel, but you are still not Ivan the Terrible, and in your heart you envy him. For you will not be able to kill your own son. Torture him, yes, but not kill. You are a Georgian. And with you, as with Jews, there is a strong feeling for blood ties. You could exterminate the whole Russian people, but you would not lay a finger on me. From that point of view, as a tyrant, historically you are inferior."

After these words Stalin seemed completely off balance. "What did you say? Kind people, did you hear what this idiot just said? He is philosophizing."

"You drove mama with your enraptured terror to . . . she shot herself."

Stalin picked up the film script and hurled it at Vasily.

'Villain!'' he yelled. "Get out of here. I don't want any part of you! Out!"

Vasily bent over, picked up the film script and put it on the table. Then he said:

"Batya, you would be better off signing the order to give your son, the son of Stalin, the title of general of the Air Force. I would disappear of my own free will. Understand?"

Stalin was still in a rage. "You are a bloody parasite, Vas'ka!"

"Again, Vas'ka. Listen old man, I honestly do not have the time to ramble on with you right now. My eagles are waiting for me at the stadium. Football training. Do you know what kind of business that is? It is big business, batya. You have said yourself that 'facts are a stubborn thing.' And the fact is that you are my father, and I am your son. You cannot change that. We are tied together by blood."

Stalin sighed. "You are an unconscionable cynic."

"That comes to me from my father," said Vasily.

"Eh," said Stalin, "my first son, Yakov Dzhugashvili . . . he was a man."

"Yasha hated you. He refused the name Stalin."

"Maybe Yakov did hate me, but he was a man." Stalin sat down heavily on the couch.

"Yakov was personally against the Soviet regime," Vasily said.

"Are *you* for it?"

"Me? I put up with it, batya."

"And you pay the party dues." Stalin's tone was ironic.

"Yes, I pay. Your Yakov even attempted suicide, with a gun," Vasily said. "Your Yakov went to war, surrendered himself to the Germans, and anti-Stalinist leaflets with his signature were scattered all over the front."

Stalin put his hands to his face for a few seconds. Then, frowning, he looked at Vasily.

"The Fascists shot Yakov," he said.

"That is presumed," Vasily said. "Nothing is known for sure. Maybe he is working as first deputy for President Truman."

"Shut up, you idiot!"

"Your Yakov was a traitor. That's what." Vasily would not let up.

"Do not uncover my wounds." Stalin was almost pleading.

"Then, batya, make me a general. Old man, all you have to do is sign a piece of paper. My situation is absolutely indecent." Vasily came to sit beside his father. "Think of your own prestige. Look at the children of our neighboring greats. Churchill's son or Roosevelt's son. They are respected."

"Do they have their own football teams?"

"Dammit batya, you must understand. I am in the position of a czarevich, but my insignia is that of a colonel. Is that the way it should be? No, it is not."

"Czarevich?" Stalin could not believe his ears, "You, a czarevich?" Then he said, more gently, "Wait a minute, son. Did you reach that conclusion all by yourself?"

"I swear in the name of the party," Vasily said. "The parallel is drawn between you and Peter the Great, all over the world. And if you are Czar Peter the Great, then I am Czarevich Alexei. Is that clear?"

"Yes, it's clear."

"Automatically, batya."

"Yes."

Vasily said in a self-satisfied way:

"You have finally come to your senses, old man."

Stalin rose, put his hands at his sides, and talked as though addressing someone beyond Vasily.

"Kind people, look at what a son Peter the Great, or rather I, have. Listen, Alexei Petrovich, wouldn't you like to be the secretary general of the Central Committee of the Soviet Communist Party, too?"

Vasily tried to make out whether his father was kidding or serious; probably he was serious.

"No, that is not for me, batya. I am a military man. Right! Left! About face! That's for me. Make me general and appoint me commander of the Air Force in the Moscow Military District. That is in your interest. I am your son. You can depend on me. Without Stalin, who am I? Nobody. Zero. If anything happens, it would be easy for you to run off, I mean to *fly* off, to some faraway place, like Chile. I could keep a jet ready. Twenty-four hours, around the clock. I could also bomb the hell out of the Kremlin, our so-called socialist citadel. At your command, of course. After all, you don't arrest your henchmen for nothing . . . from time to time."

"Fly, you say? To Chile?"

"Yes, to Chile. What's wrong with that?"

"Not a bad idea, that's what," said Stalin, and he laughed. His laughter was contagious. Father and son laughed together. Then the son extended his hand.

"Well, batya, shall we shake on it?"

"I'll tell you what I will do," Stalin said, "I will expel you from the Communist party, strip you of your rank, and send you somewhere to the Kurils. Not to Chile, but to the Kurils. Have you heard of those islands, son?"

"Have I heard of the Kuril Islands? You bit them off from Japan."

"They miss you in the Kurils, Vasily, oh how they miss you."

A frown appeared on Vasily's face.

"Are you serious?"

"You won't play football in the Kurils."

"For the last time, will you make me a general or not?"

"The Russian people say: 'Do not count, Ivan, on the pocket of another man.' "

"You've stuffed yourself with Russian proverbs. All right. I've had it with you. Enough. With my best Communist regards, goodbye, leader of the people!"

Vasily moved toward the door. Stalin's eyes glittered and he shouted after his son:

"Turn around!"

Reflexively, Vasily turned on his heels, almost falling to the floor. Recovering, he held his arms against his sides. Stalin, calmer now, said:

"You will spend ten nights in the guardhouse, Comrade Colonel."

"Batya, have you gone mad?"

Stalin looked at him coldly.

"Repeat the order!"

Vasily was a military man and his military habits were stronger than all others.

"Ten nights in the guardhouse, Comrade Generalissimo of the Soviet Union!" he shouted. "I will carry out the order, Comrade Generalissimo of the Soviet Union."

"Turn around!"

This time Vasily turned on his heels more accurately and when his father said "March!" he walked with only a slight stagger. As he opened the door and disappeared, Stalin shook his head and said to himself, "He will fall somewhere, the drunk, and mess up his face. Ah, children, children . . ."

Stalin paced the living room, then returned to the couch and sat down. Reaching for the film script, he opened it and began reading.

Several minutes later, Beria came into the room. He was in civilian dress, which hung on him like a sack, and his tie was crooked.

"Good evening, Josif Vissarionovich. May I, batono?"

"What do you want?" Stalin did not look up.

Beria stood at a respectful distance.

"You ask what I want," he said. "Well, I will tell you, Josif Vissarionovich. You have hurt your own son. Does a Georgian do that? Colonel Stalin cried."

"Cried?" Stalin looked up and grinned. "Does that scum really cry?"

"Indeed he does, Josif Vissarionovich!"

"Beria, he's a drunk," Stalin said. "In addition, he's not Colonel Stalin, he's *General* Stalin."

"What?"

Stalin went to the Kremlin telephone, picked up the receiver, dialed a number, and said:

"Comrade Poskrebyshev? Listen carefully. In the interest of strengthening our great armed forces, I think that Colonel Stalin should be awarded the title of major-general of the Air Force, and simultaneously appointed as commander of the Air Force of the Moscow Military District."

After he had hung up, Beria asked, "Should I reverse the ten days in the guardhouse?"

"No, don't," Stalin said. "He'll be smarter when he gets out. By the way, Beria, have you heard of a country called Chile?"

"Of course," said Beria. "I think it's in Argentina. Either that, or Argentina is in Chile. One or the other. Is something bothering you?"

"Mmmmm . . ." Stalin murmured. "Not yet."

"If you would like, Josif Vissarionovich . . ."

"You will arrange a revolution there?" Stalin smiled. "Or perhaps you can just cover up Chile? Erase it from the map? You are a master in your field, Comrade Beria. But unfortunately there are things in this world that are beyond our control. . . . I wish to God that I were wrong, Beria."

"But I think that everything in this world—everything—depends on the will of Comrade Stalin."

Stalin opened up the film script, and searched until he found a certain passage.

"Vas'ka was probably right. Two or three words should be added. In this place. It should read: 'In the never-ending fields of Russia, our dear teacher, the great Stalin appeared.' What do you think, Comrade Beria?"

The Jewish Question

On that particular night I went to the Moscow Art Theatre because Stalin was attending a performance of his favorite play, *The Days of the Turbins* (about the czarist White Army officers, of all things). During the first intermission I went to the government box with its bulletproof walls. In the anteroom, the leader was eating roasted nuts and being entertained by General Vlasek, a rare idiot, fat, with the face of a butcher. Formerly a mere soldier, Vlasek now received a second salary as Stalin's personal photographer. He was showing Stalin some photographs.

When Stalin saw me, he stopped chewing on the nuts and asked:

"Well, Beria? Did you clear it up? What does he wear, sideburns or earlocks?"

I glanced at Vlasek. Stalin understood my meaning and told him to leave. After Vlasek had left the room, I said to Stalin:

"Josif Vissarionovich, my specialists assure me that he wears earlocks. But he maintains that he wears sideburns."

"That means it's still not clear."

I tried to justify myself. "Josif Vissarionovich, this is a very delicate question."

Stalin got up from the sofa and said rudely:

"That's all I need. A relative with earlocks. It's not enough that he's the head of an administrative division."

"Yes, but he's head of the administrative division of the Institute of Experimental Physiology at the Academy of Sciences of the USSR."

"What difference does that make? All the heads of administrative divisions are crooks." Stalin began to pace the room, swinging his good arm, the right one, slightly.

"Yes, that's right, Josif Vissarionovich, all the heads of administrative divisions are crooks."

"What ever possessed Svetlana! Isn't it enough that her fiancé is a Jew? But, no, her fiancé's father turns out to be a crook with earlocks."

I couldn't help myself and burst out laughing. "A crook with earlocks."

"You may laugh, Beria, but I am just unlucky, unlucky, do you understand." Stalin seemed to be asking for sympathy.

I smacked my lips.

"Luckiness and unluckiness each have their turn, Josif Vissarionovich, batono."

Stalin stopped pacing and said one word: Moroz.* Moroz was the last name of his daughter's fiancé. And it was a name that sent shivers up and down Stalin's spine.

"What should I do?" Stalin asked.

---

* The Russian word for frost.

I tried to second-guess the leader's thoughts and, as usual, began with the most extreme suggestion.

"Shall we arrest them both?"

"The father and the son?"

"Just give me the word, Josif Vissarionovich."

Stalin brushed me aside with his right arm and said:

"All you want to do is arrest, Beria. You can always arrest. But we must think of something else."

I sat down on a chair, took off my pince-nez and started to clean them with my handkerchief. I had been occupied with Svetlana's marriage for over a week. This was a matter of state importance. I had set everything else aside. It is not a laughing matter when the daughter of the leader gets married.

Stalin again began to pace. He scratched his mustache and then said:

"He undoubtedly plays chess. A champion, probably?"

"The father?"

"The son, Moroz the younger. What is his name, Gregori or something?"

I shook my head and said that it was strange but Moroz the younger, according to my information, did not play chess. However, he was a good Ping-Pong player. This amazed Stalin.

"That isn't a Jewish game."

I waved my arms and said:

"The younger generation, Josif Vissarionovich, they are breaking away from the traditions of their fathers."

"Is he a skirt chaser?"

I said that Moroz did not have that reputation. Then Stalin recalled how several years before we had arrested and sent to a labor camp a screen writer who was trying to turn Svetlana's head. Stalin emphasized that he also was a Jew.

"We send such persons to Stalin's corrective-labor camps," he said. "That kind needs to have his brain fixed. Is that not right, Beria?"

"And we fix their brains, Comrade Stalin," I answered solemnly.

Stalin lit one of his cigarettes and sat down on the sofa.

"According to your facts, Beria, this Gregori Moroz is simply a harmless Soviet Jew. Right?"

I nodded. But Stalin abruptly returned to the father's earlocks. At this point I made a suggestion.

"If you order it, we can shave them off."

Stalin looked at me questioningly and asked in disbelief: "Forcibly? Have you lost your mind? No, you cannot do that. I categorically forbid it. That would be an encroachment on national tradition. But if he himself . . ."

"We will exert our influence," I said.

"That is a different matter," Stalin replied. "Communism, Lavrenti Pavlovich, is an idea. And in this world of ideas, it is important to know how to influence."

"We will exert our influence. You may consider the fiancé's father without earlocks."

"In that case, he will have to be appointed deputy to the director of that institute. What's it called?"

"The Institute of Experimental Physiology."

Stalin asked whether there was a vacancy. I assured him that it would be arranged. He was cheered up. One part of the problem was solved. But the main question remained: the last name. At this point I mentioned that my specialists felt that Moroz could have been a Belorussian name and that several people by that name had been uncovered in the Ukraine.

Stalin again grew angry and said:

"A lot your specialists understand. This Moroz is a Jew.

The name Moroz is, of course, Jewish. Stalin, as you well know, is the leader of the *international* proletariat. For that reason, it is not as simple as you think. Another thing, Beria, the Jewish people are a great people and their contribution to the culture of mankind is immense. I would even say gigantic. As for the fact that the Jews are called the chosen people, in the opinion of the leader of the international proletariat, that is Comrade Stalin, there has been an attempt throughout Jewish history to conceal the class division and class struggle among Jews with this stupid legend. That is how the rabbis and damned Zionists want to limit the social consciousness of the working masses."

Having completed this short speech, Stalin apparently decided to test my knowledge of the history of the Jewish people.

"Beria, do you know when the first synagogue in the world was built?"

"Do what you like with me, I don't know," I answered.

"That is bad, Comrade Beria, very bad." The leader reproached me with a slight smile.

I apologized, explaining that I had not been taught Jewish history in school and university.

"It was built around 400 B.C."

"Really? I never would have thought so."

"And Beria, do you know who Nebuchadnezzar was?"

"Do what you like, I do not know," I admitted. It could be very dangerous to lie to Stalin.

"A Babylonian czar!" Stalin said and added: "He invaded Jerusalem, sacked it and took the Jews into captivity."

"What a scoundrel!" I cried out involuntarily.

"What did you say, Beria?"

I decided that I had made a mistake and immediately backtracked by saying: "Perhaps he was a progressive man,

Josif Vissarionovich. But your erudition amazes me. You know everything!''

"And why do Jews eat matzos, Beria?" Stalin continued.

"They *ate* matzos," I answered immediately, "they used to eat them. Now they eat white bread. Matzos are forbidden in the USSR, Josif Vissarionovich."

"Really? Who forbade them? That is disgraceful. Why are Georgians allowed to eat their Georgian bread, tornispuri, and Jews are not allowed to eat their matzos? Who forbade them, I ask?"

What could I do but tell the truth?

"I beg your pardon . . . you, Comrade Stalin."

He was not at all embarrassed. He simply said: "That's right, Comrade Beria, that's right. It's better that way. The nationality question is a ticklish one. I know it inside out. All the traditions, rituals, and so on. By the way, I think perhaps all Soviet Jews should be sent to, let's say . . . the Crimea. And they like fruit, resorts, palms."

I agreed. "Just give the orders, Josif Vissarionovich, and it will be done."

Stalin began to laugh.

"There used to be Moscow Jews. One, two, three, and they became Crimean Jews. Only this should not be a step toward a kind of Jewish ghetto. Under no circumstances. This should be a preventive measure, so to speak. A certain amount of autonomy will be useful for both the Russian and the Jewish people. But as it is, the Russians are complaining about Jewish dominance. Is that not so?"

"Yes," I answered. "Only . . ."

"Only what?"

"I feel sorry for Crimea," I answered frankly.

Stalin agreed with me.

"Yes, so do I. But they won't go to Murmansk. In a word, Comrade Beria, it's necessary to weigh all the choices. Think the organizational measures through, so this won't look like a deportation. The Jews should express their desire *themselves*. Do you understand?"

"Of course, Comrade Stalin. They will express their own desires."

"They are also builders of communism, Beria!"

How could I deny that? I couldn't, so I said with 100-percent confidence:

"Under your wise leadership, leader."

Five minutes remained before the second act, and Stalin returned to Moroz. The question of his name remained unsolved.

"Let us analyze the situation more thoroughly, Beria," said Stalin. "As I have already noted, Comrade Stalin is the leader of the international proletariat, and therefore, along with the international proletariat, he should treat Jews— how should I put it—carefully. Exactly so. *Carefully*. Often, Beria, I must, as the leader of the international proletariat, subordinate my private interests and tastes to the interests and tastes of the masses. And so we must deal with prejudices peculiar to the international proletariat. I ask you: Will this proletariat be pleased to know that Comrade Stalin's son-in-law is a Jew? What do you think, Beria?"

"No, the international proletariat will not be pleased."

"Yes, yes. Therefore, let us do the following: Let us change Moroz to Morozov. We will add just two letters to the name. Morozov is a good Russian name. And everything will fit into place."

In cases such as this Stalin amazed me at every turn. He had a special ability to solve problems in his own way, approaching them from the most unlikely angle and coming up with the most unexpected solutions.

"How? By changing the last name?" I asked.

"And why not?"

Stalin had decided to baptize his son-in-law. Just like that. I could not help laughing.

"Stalin's baptismal."

"That's right," Stalin agreed. "Only it must be done secretly, so that no rumors are spread."

"But how will Svetlana take this?"

"Comrade Beria, I love my daughter, but there are times when the leader of the international proletariat must consider *only* the interests of the international proletariat. Is that clear?"

I was delighted. The most complex things can, in fact, be so easy. Only a genius would make the decision to baptize his own son-in-law from the Jew Moroz to the Russian Morozov. This was a wonder. One more of Stalin's wonders.

My delight angered the leader. He frowned and said,

"You have somehow lost control, Beria. You should be working, Comrade Beria, not showing your teeth. History will not forgive chatter. We are Bolsheviks, Comrade Beria. Do not forget that, please. And warn my son-in-law and his father that if they reveal this government secret, we will . . ."

"Arrest them," I said.

Stalin nodded, took a roasted nut from the plate, put it in his mouth, and left for his box to see the second act of *The Days of the Turbins*.

As he left, I heard him sigh deeply and say to himself: "Ah, these damned Jews, there is no getting away from them."

The Game of Billiards

Beria knew that he had to lose to Stalin, which he did, even though Stalin sometimes would notice and get angry. Once, out of curiosity, Beria decided to win. . . . It happened at pocket billiards.

Billiards was for Stalin not only a pastime, but a necessity as well. Doctors had been concerned for a long time because his left hand had begun to shrink. The problem of what was wrong with this hand, by the way, has never been solved. Most probably, it had been injured in childhood. And so, because of orders from the infamous doctors (Stalin had a lifelong dislike of doctors), the leader had a steam bath twice a week in the one specially built for him at Blizhnaya. Afterward he would play billiards, usually with billiard-scorer Akhmet, a little old Tatar who had hair on his fingers. During the game they would converse, of course, sometimes about "life," and Stalin would complain to Akhmet about "those Bolsheviks" and "the cretins" in the Central Committee. He would sigh then and say something like:

"Ah, Akhmet, what those idiots in the Central Committee won't think of! How can you people live with these Bolshevik sons of bitches? You can't make a move without their surveillance."

Akhmet would diplomatically keep silent. But once Akhmet advised the leader to lower the price of foodstuffs and manufactured goods. And afterward Stalin did, indeed, by the decision of the Council of Ministers and the Central Committee of the Soviet Communist party, lower the price of salt, matches and bicycles on the average of 2 to 5 percent.

So we come to that time when he was playing billiards with Beria. Stalin soon realized that he was going to lose, and he began to smile and praise Beria.

"You have the hand of a strong man, Lavrenti Pavlovich," he said. "It's a pleasure to watch you sink the balls in the pockets, as though they weren't balls but human skulls."

Beria took this as a compliment and sank another ball. The better he played, the more Stalin smiled and extolled him. And Beria almost decided to win from that point on. At the end of the game Stalin said:

"Is it permissible to ask, Comrade Beria, whether it is true that when you were a young officer in the state security in Georgia, you followed pretty women around, lured them into gateways and dark entryways and mauled them, threatening them with your frightening title when necessary?"

Beria was embarrassed because this was true, although he of course denied it and insisted that the story was slander and insinuation. Since his arrival in Moscow, Beria had tried to control all channels of information to Stalin other than himself. But Stalin managed to find out a great deal on his own, which drove Beria to his wit's end. And this particularly delighted the leader.

That evening, Stalin invited Beria to stay for dinner. They drank a wine called Alexandrauly, which the leader preferred above all others and which was specially filtered in a special shop of one of the wine distilleries in Moscow, under the state security surveillance. They ate chicken "tabaka" made by Stalin himself, and Georgian bread, of course. As always, Beria pleased Stalin with his anecdotes, of which he had an inexhaustible supply without repeating himself. On this occasion, Beria told about the old Georgian who willed his son the sacred goblet, saying:

"My son, I have drunk a whole tank of wine from this goblet. Now you drink, but drink only from this side." And the old man pointed to the edge closest to him. "Never drink from the other side."

"Father, why?" asked his son.

"Oh, what a fool you are, my son," said the old man. "Look, if you drink from the other side, the wine will spill on your knees rather than in your mouth."

Beria took an empty glass and demonstrated this to Stalin.

It was a stupid joke, but the leader laughed.

Then they sang together. Beria knew many Georgian songs and was very musical. Stalin had a small but pleasant voice. He had sung in the choir during his years at the seminary.

They stayed up until midnight. And during this time, the leader did not bring up the billiard game once. When the clock struck twelve, he said:

"Now let us go to Moscow and work."

Stalin took Beria in his own limousine, so that the marshal's "cavalcade" of two cars followed the leader's, but without Beria. Stalin brought Beria into his private room in the Kremlin, sat him in a chair, and went to the safe. All this was done without explanation and Beria was uneasily expecting a dirty trick.

After Stalin had opened the safe and dug around in it for a while, he took out several sheets of paper and glanced over their contents. Then he smiled as he approached Beria and sat down across from him.

"Here, Comrade Beria, I have wanted to acquaint you with these two documents for a long time. Hold on and don't interrupt me. O.K.?"

"O.K.," Beria answered, lowering his head into his shoulders and preparing himself for the attack.

Without hurrying, as though he were relishing every word, Stalin read the following to the marshal:

"On Saturday, August 22, at the invitation of Lavrenti Beria, I went to his *dacha* in Gagry. After lunch he suggested a ride in his motorboat. The guards watched from shore. Beria stripped down to his underclothes. I did the same. We got into the powerful boat and in ten minutes were out on the Black Sea.

"Beria suddenly noticed a swimmer. When we approached, the swimmer turned out to be a woman. She was a record-holding swimmer, who was doing her training in preparation for the All-Soviet Competition. Her name was Masha Dratvina, and she was on the Dynamo team. Beria stopped the boat and began talking with her. She recognized the marshal and lost her composure. Lavrenti then pulled her on board. He examined her with his eyes and said to me in Georgian: 'Look, Vovka, what a beauty, what breasts, and what hips. Lovely!' And he added: 'Here's what,

Vovka, you dive into the water and swim to shore, because I want to make love to Masha here on the boat.'

"It was three miles to shore, and I barely knew how to swim. I mentioned this to Lavrenti. He became angry and turned on the motor, moving the boat one or two miles closer to shore. Then he picked me up without a word and threw me into the water. In a few minutes I began to drown. Luckily, Beria's guards noticed all of this from shore—they were watching their boss through binoculars—and a second boat came to my rescue. They barely revived me. After the supper, at which Lavrenti's wife, Nina, and son, Sergo, were present, we went to play billiards. Beria said to me: 'You know, Vovka, this Masha is so temperamental, so passionate. We had quite a time. I have a date with her for tomorrow in the same place, in the open sea.' "

Beria leaned his head back in the chair. Stalin paused in his reading, then repeated:

"In the open sea. May I ask you, Comrade Beria, what would have happened if this Vovka had drowned in the Black Sea? Eh? Probably you would have sent a wreath with a note reading: 'To Vovka, the Georgian professor, the philosopher, who tragically drowned while on government duty, from Marshal Lavrenti Beria.' Right?"

Beria did not answer. He was cursing his boyhood chum, Vovka, to himself three times over for so cheaply betraying him.

"I will now read you another document, Comrade Beria." Again Stalin read slowly, as though he were relishing every word.

"As the chairman of the Committee of Physical Culture and Athletics in Georgia, I presented, and still present to Marshal Lavrenti Beria, young female gymnasts. I was not able to refuse this duty, for then Marshal Beria would have sent me to Siberia or somewhere even farther away. Moreover, as a dedicated Communist, I consider girls as trivia in comparison with the great government work that Beria carries out. The question of his physical well-being is of the utmost importance.

"This special duty began when I brought our first Georgian delegation to Moscow, to the parade on Soviet Athletics Day. The chief of Beria's secretariat called me to say that the marshal invited me and my Georgian athletes to his *dacha*. He hinted that Beria liked plump young women. I picked out some plump ones and we set out for Beria's *dacha*. The marshal presented us with a magnificent dinner. Everyone drank too much. Beria then spent the night with one of the Georgian gymnasts. After that, a regular pattern was established. Each year, on Soviet Athletics Day, I selected two or three plump young women for the marshal and drove them out to his *dacha*. Occasionally, he selected some additional ones himself, right at the parade on Red Square, while he was standing on the platform of the Lenin Mausoleum next to the great Stalin. The chief of the marshal's secretariat would call me after the parade and say: 'Bring the fourth from the left in the front row, and the third from the right in the second row.' And I brought the one from the first row and the one from the second row. Occasionally I made a mistake and was reprimanded.

"I should add that all the technical matters were decided by the head of Beria's guards. According to my information, Marshal Beria actually has two of them. The first, Nadoraja, is in charge of security, and the second, Sarkisov, is in charge of 'women affairs.' I was told that in the state security apparatus this one is called 'the head of the marshal's harem.' I was also told that Beria would point out some woman from the windows of his car, and Sarkisov would get out of the car and salute her and say 'Colonel Sarkisov, of the state security, from Marshal Beria's guards. . . .'' This of course made an impression and rarely did these women refuse a meeting with Beria.''

Stalin lowered the paper, looked at Beria, and said:

"Try to refuse and he'll arrest you. Well, it's frightening. Marshal Beria himself, the head of state security, dammit!''

Beria did not answer.

"Do you understand, marshal,'' Stalin went on, "what will happen to you if I make these two documents known to the Politburo? Suppose I add to these documents the fact that you have dozens of illegitimate children in Moscow and that on special occasions at the state security club you pick out your victims in succession, the daughters of your generals, and the generals dutifully present them to you, dammit. But don't try to get even with this Vovka or with the chairman of the Committee on Physical Culture and Athletics. If you touch them, you will have to deal with me. Is that clear?''

Completely devastated, Beria left for his ministry. He thought that his career was over, that Stalin had a stranglehold on him and that there was no way out. He even considered suicide, but at the same time he felt a glimmer of hope because Stalin had known of his sexual escapades for a long time and these documents probably had been in the safe for many months. Of course when Stalin had returned the documents to the safe, he had taken out several arrest forms, signed by the general procurator, stamped and sealed. And these were orders of the leader to arrest Molotov, Voroshilov, Kaganovich, and Khrushchev.

"They could disappear any day," Stalin had said. "Their lives hang by a thread. Molotov is connected, after all, with American Zionists, through his wife, and Voroshilov worked for the Germans. As far as Khrushchev is concerned, he is a well-known Polish spy."

Beria knew that the leader had prepared orders for the arrest of all his comrades and disciples, and that he, Beria, was perhaps among them.

The marshal sat in his enormous study with the windows looking out on the Lubyanka, and gazed at the huge portrait of the great leader that hung before him on the wall. He whispered:

"If only you would die, you old turkey. If only you would die . . ."

Suddenly the phone rang, the one that was connected only to the members of the Politburo. Beria picked up the receiver and heard Stalin's voice:

"You know, Beria, I had the thought that if Ivan IV had been smarter and had liquidated two or three hundred more boyar families, the Russians would not have had a Time of Troubles. Remember that in your future work."

Stalin liked to say this about Ivan IV, about the boyars, and about the Time of Troubles. But Beria's spirits revived. This meant that there would be no repercussions because of what had transpired in Stalin's private room.

"Dammit," said Beria, when the conversation with Stalin was over. "Did I have to be such an idiot and win that game!"

Koba

Very few who landed in a concentration camp under Stalin got out alive, to say nothing of being rehabilitated. There were some lucky ones. One, two, five.

Among them was Sergo, an old Bolshevik and comrade in arms to Stalin.

One fine day, seemingly as if by magic, Sergo appeared at Stalin's *dacha* in Kuntsevo. Here he met his wife, Sopha, who had been freed from another concentration camp and brought to Stalin's *dacha,* also as if by magic. These two were not young any more; they were emaciated, but decently dressed.

"Sopha! Sophochka . . . is that you?" Sergo cried.

"Sergo . . ." She fell into his arms.

They had not seen each other since the day of their arrest in 1937, twelve years before. Twelve whole years.

"You are gray, Sopha. Were you also in exile?"

She nodded, and wiped the tears from her eyes.

"My dearest, I thought you were dead."

"No, no, I am alive. And we are together. But where

are we? Where are we, Sopha?'' Sergo looked around.

At this moment Stalin walked into the room, followed by Beria. Stalin was clean-shaven, in the full dress of the generalissimo, and looked neat and cheerful. Beria was wearing a dark civilian suit.

"Here you are together again, friends.'' Stalin said.

"Koba! Soso!'' Sergo and Sopha exclaimed in unison.

Koba, a people's hero in Georgian history, was Stalin's revolutionary name, and Soso was short for Josif. His close friends from Georgia called him Soso, but of those there were few left. Most who could call him Soso had ended up in camps after 1937 or were shot, by order of the leader or in spite of him, which is how he liked to think of it.

"Hello, Sergo. Hello, Sopha.'' Stalin spoke in Georgian.

Sergo hugged Stalin and kissed him on both cheeks.

"Koba, was it you who did it?''

"What, exactly? Reuniting a husband and wife? Are you against that, Sergo?''

"I am ready to kiss your feet,'' Sergo said passionately.

"We will do without that, Sergo. There are no accountings between old revolutionary friends. You suffered in 1937. That crazy state security executioner, Ezhov, arrested everyone. You got in his path in error, and your wife too. . .''

Sopha asked, "Where is our daughter, Soso?''

"Tomorrow she will be in Moscow and you can see her. By mistake the state security generals did not see to it that she was brought today. I have already reprimanded Beria. He now has Ezhov's position. Do you remember him, Sergo?''

"Of course, of course,'' Sergo said. "Secretary of the Transcaucasian Communist party Committee.''

"How do you do, batono, Sergo," said Beria with dignity, extending his hand.

"I am pleased to see you, Comrade Beria." Sergo shook Beria's hand.

Sopha clasped her hand to her gray head. She was practically choking from happiness.

"That means that Maika will be with us tomorrow! And for long, Soso?"

"Forever!" Stalin declared.

"This is all like a fairy tale." Tears again appeared in Sopha's eyes.

"No, friends, it is all very simple. It is all according to the law of dialectics," said Stalin. "Not too long ago, Sergo, I came across your letter in my archives, dated January 1917. You were then in Poti, on the Black Sea. On party assignment. I remembered you and ordered Beria to find you, to hold a new investigation, so that you could be freed. I was convinced that you were incapable of committing any crime against your party."

Sergo, who was short and stocky, stretched up like a rooster and said solemnly:

"For me, the party comes before everything else."

"Sit down, Sopha," Stalin said politely and indicated a chair. "The Russian people say: 'There is no truth in legs.' Is that not so?"

"Yes, but it is very hard for me to leave Sergo's side. I have not seen him in so many years."

Sergo nodded in agreement. "Very many years, Koba."

"I know. I am sorry for that, Sergo." Stalin finished that sentence rather dryly, adding, "It was necessary, probably, for the country to go through that meat grinder."

"Preventive measures are necessary even now, Josif Vissarionovich,'' Beria said decisively. "There are still many class enemies.''

"All right, all right, let us not bring up the past,'' Stalin said irritably.

"You have not changed at all, Koba,'' Sergo began enthusiastically. "The same Abrek!* Remember in jail, in Baku, how we called you Jaures after the French revolutionary Jaures?''

Stalin laughed and placed his right hand against the edge of his tunic as Napolean Bonaparte had done.

"There was that matter. There was a jail. There was Baku. There was all that and it is all gone now. And Jaures, Sergo, I have left a long way behind. In world history books, he will be somewhere at the bottom of the list of reformers, while I . . . I will probably be somewhere next to Lenin.''

"Undoubtedly, Josif Vissarionovich, batono,'' Beria interjected.

"Of course, of course,'' Sergo agreed quickly.

"I am no longer fit for the Abrek, Sergo. I am too old.'' Stalin said this in such a way that Sergo and Beria had to disagree immediately.

"No, Koba, do not say that. We Georgians are a long-lived people. Our ancestors lived to be a hundred and we will live to be a hundred,'' Sergo asserted.

"Of course,'' Beria said.

Stalin again laughed and turned to Sopha:

"They are obviously out to please Comrade Stalin, aren't they?'' Without waiting for her answer, he added: "Sergo, you look wonderful. My God! Look at him, Comrade Beria. He's a perfect advertisement for your corrective-

* Caucasian rider.

labor camps. This man spent twelve years in Siberia, probably on the taiga, and he's pink as a suckling pig, fresh as a
cucumber. Sopha, don't you think your husband looks magnificent despite his ordeal?''

"Thank the Lord, Soso," Sopha answered. "I don't
know about his camp, but life in mine was no picnic. They
started to fatten me up three weeks before I came to Moscow. Probably at your order, Comrade Beria.''

Stalin obviously sensed a reproach in Sopha's words, for
he said: "If you have any complaints. . . .''

"What kind of complaints could we have, Koba?" Sergo
interrupted. "Camp is camp, of course, it's not paradise.
But this was a *Soviet* camp, and that's why I accepted the
hardships and inconveniences as just and lawful. That is
how it should be in a socialistic society.''

"Well said, Sergo. Good fellow!" Stalin sat down on the
couch. "Sit next to me, Sergo.''

"Thank you!''

"Soso, where are we?" Sopha ventured to ask. "In the
Kremlin? Or on a *dacha?* I'm in the dark. After being freed
from camp, I was washed, my hair was cut, I was dressed in
these clothes, and put on a military plane. I flew the whole
day, I think. Then I was taken from the airfield to a car with
covered windows.''

"Don't worry, Sopha," Stalin said. "We are at a *dacha*
on the outskirts of Moscow. But don't think that I have
become a landowner. This is not the property of Comrade
Stalin. This is state property. Please help yourself, Sopha,
there is fruit on the table. Georgian fruit. Beria gets it directly from Tbilisi, by air.''

"We expose it to special irradiation," Beria said
proudly, "in order to kill the bacteria." Sergo rested his

right hand on Stalin's shoulder in a comradely manner, as he had done half a century earlier, and asked:

"How are your children, Koba? How are Svetlana, Vasily, and Yakov?"

"The Germans captured Yakov and shot him," the leader said, lowering his head.

"That can't be!" Sergo cried.

"We can't find the grave to this day. I have offered a reward of one million roubles. I have a great deal of money now. Author's fees, for my books." Stalin seemed to be justifying his wealth.

"How very sad, Soso. Yakov was a good boy."

"Vasily is a general of the Air Force," Stalin continued. "A commander." He paused. "Svetlana married. I have a grandson. Even though he is a Jew." He finished the sentence with a slight smile on his lips.

"Congratulations, grandfather," Sopha said as she sat down.

Now Beria alone was on his feet, apparently not wanting to take a seat without Stalin's permission.

"And how is your mother?" Sergo inquired.

"She believed in God until the very last day and wore that idiotic religious garb," Stalin said. "The mother of the leader of the international proletariat in a religious costume! How do you like that?"

"Your first wife also believed in God," Sopha said boldly.

"My first wife was a child." Stalin seemed slightly embarrassed. "How can you compare her with my mother, the old witch!"

"Oh, Soso, don't speak like that of your own mother!" Sopha was almost shocked.

"And why not?" Stalin asked coldly. "I am not an English lord or diplomat. I do not hide this. Do you know why I did not go to Tbilisi during the last years? I was afraid of meeting her, my own mother, because, for God's sake, she might have poisoned her own son, the atheist and Bolshevik."

Sergo felt that it was time to change the subject.

"Koba, you know that the war passed me by. I was in camp all that time. I knew something from old newspapers and from the radio. We had a radio in our barracks. Did you, Sopha?"

"Yes, we even organized political discussions," Sopha said, not without irony.

"Political discussions in corrective-labor camps are essential." This from Beria.

"Don't talk too much," Stalin said with a frown.

"I heard that you received the important title of generalissimo of the Soviet Union," Sergo continued.

"Received?" Stalin asked. "No, I gave it to myself. That would be more accurate. It's quite an honor, you know. Generalissimo. There are only three in the world. Me, Chiang Kai-shek, and Franco. The company, as you can see, is questionable."

"Why put yourself among them?"

Stalin seemed not to hear this. "You will have to work hard now, Sergo. You will have to read a great deal, travel around the country, observe. You will have to make up for those twelve tragic years. You will learn much and see much. The Soviet Union, despite the last war, has made enormous progress."

"Koba, may I count myself a member of our dear Communist, Leninist, Stalinist party?"

"You may, Sergo. Comrade Beria, give Sergo his party document."

"With pleasure, batono."

Beria took Sergo's party membership card from his pocket and gave it to him. In addition, he had two passports, prepared in advance, of course, which he gave to Sergo and Sopha.

"Are you pleased, Sergo?" Stalin asked.

Sergo kissed the membership card.

"Long live Comrade Stalin!"

"Very well, very well, you are happy, I see. Now let's get down to business. Listen to me carefully, Sergo." Stalin was speaking with his famous pauses. "I must, of course, apologize for assigning you a job without first asking your approval."

"In Georgia?"

"No," answered Stalin. "I want to have you at my side here in Moscow. By the decision of the Secretariat of the Central Committee, you are, as of tomorrow, deputy minister of foreign affairs of the USSR."

Sopha was the first to recover from the shock of this statement.

"Did I hear you correctly, Soso? You said deputy minister of foreign affairs of the USSR?"

"Isn't that enough?"

"It's enough, it's enough!" Sergo shouted, crazed with joy.

"I am no longer amazed by anything," Sopha said as she ran to Sergo. She hugged him and kissed him, and then asked, "But how will you manage? You will have to prove worthy of Comrade Stalin's trust in you."

"He will manage, Sopha, he will manage," Stalin answered her. "There are not many intelligent people among

my ministers and deputy ministers. There are many dull-
ards. Of course, I would not say that of Beria."

"Thank you, Josif Vissarionovich, batono."

"This one has the czar in his head," Stalin added mean-
ingfully.

Beria laughed it off. "How should I interpret that, Josif
Vissarionovich? I am not a monarchist."

"Work as a deputy for a year or two, Sergo, and I will
put you in Molotov's position. Molotov is a fool and I am
tired of him. Beria, don't tell Molotov about this or he'll
come to me in tears again. His eyes are often wet with tears,
dammit, and he even took part in the October Revolution
along with me and Lenin."

"What are you saying! What are you saying, Koba!"
Sergo exclaimed.

"That's only the beginning," Stalin said. "If you don't
like Molotov's job I will make you an ambassador, let's say
to Rumania. You will be in full charge there. Rumania is
our so-called satellite. And if you don't like Rumania, I will
send you to another country to represent our interest."

Stalin got up from the couch and Sergo again embraced
him.

"Jaures!"

"That is past."

"Abrek!"

"Sergo—and you, Sopha—there is an apartment awaiting you. In the heart of Moscow, on Gorki Street."

"Good heavens!" Sopha's eyes were wide.

"And as far as I know, the apartment is decent," Stalin
continued. "It comes from my personally reserved quota.
Four rooms with all the conveniences. The furniture is ma-
hogany; I think it is better than mine. Your personal car is
parked by the front door, and you may use it twenty-four

hours a day. The salary is twelve thousand a month. Plus a package and a ration. What is the ration, Comrade Beria?''

"Fifteen hundred rubles a month.''

"That means that you will get fifteen hundred rubles worth of food at the Kremlin food center. More than enough for three. The doors of the Kremlin hospital are, of course, open to you and your family. And, of course, all the special favors of the government services: clothing, shoes, an allowance for literature, theater tickets. And a *dacha* in the Serebriani Bor.

"Now the package. Beria, what package is due the deputy minister of foreign affairs of the USSR?''

"Three thousand rubles a month.''

"To you, from the communist, Leninist and Stalinist party,'' Stalin went on. "These are tokens of the party, so to speak. Of course, you will get tokens from your ministry. And in time, if we choose you as a member of the Central Committee, you will get an additional ten thousand rubles a month. Is that enough?''

"Koba, what are you thinking about? Have we Bolsheviks ever been greedy?'' Sergo asked.

"We Bolsheviks are not greedy, you say. But remember, appetite develops with food.'' Stalin looked at Sopha. "And you are a minister's wife now. I know several ministers' wives. They are piranhas, Sergo. They never stop wanting things. As for you, Sopha, if you wish to work, we will arrange for you to be a French teacher at the highest school of diplomacy. I hope you did not forget French in that camp.''

"No, no,'' Sopha answered hastily. "And I will be so happy to start working again.''

"Where are Sergo's decorations, Beria?'' Stalin asked.

"Here, batono.'' Beria took a small bag from his pocket.

"These are yours, Sergo, yours." Stalin said. "You have earned them honestly. Unfortunately, they were confiscated at the time of your arrest, but you should wear these decorations, wear them with pride, because they mark your contribution to the building of socialism."

"Thank you, Comrade Stalin," Sergo said softly, as he took the small bag from Beria.

Stalin then said that everything, absolutely everything, that had been confiscated in 1937 at the time of their arrest would be returned or compensation made. This signified full and unconditional rehabilitation.

Sopha burst into tears, like a child. Her nerves had given way. She put her hands to her face, but could not control herself. Stalin nodded compassionately and looked at Sergo as though to say, it is natural for women to do this. He asked Beria to take Sopha outside and show her the flower garden.

"Shall we smoke, Sergo?" Stalin asked when they were alone.

"Yes, let's smoke, Koba."

They lit up and sat on the couch.

"Tell me, Koba, where is our revolutionary friend Budu Mdivani?" Sergo asked between puffs.

"He died in exile," Stalin answered. "You see how lucky you are."

"Wasn't he your foster brother?"

"Yes."

"And where is our revolutionary friend Mamia Orekhelashvili?"

"He also died in exile, somewhere in Siberia."

"And his wife, Maria?"

"She too . . ."

Sergo then asked cautiously:

"Koba, how about Lavrenti Kartvelishvili, the ardent Bolshevik and magnificent organizer?"

"He was shot in 1937."

"What about Levan Gogoberidze?"

"He was shot in 1937."

"And our dear comrade in arms, Lenin's favorite, Aveli Enukidze?"

"Where, where . . . in exile, shot, dead. There is nothing left of our great revolutionary cohorts except bones. You know, Sergo, the Russian people say: 'When the forest is cut, chips must fly.' And that's how it happened. You must understand that many of our former friends turned out to be cowards, traitors, factionists. The times demanded cruelty and firmness. And it is natural that under such circumstances there were excesses."

"Tell me, Koba, why did you do all this?"

"All what?"

"Well, free Sopha and me, appoint me deputy minister."

"Ah." Stalin smiled. "First of all, I trust you, as I trust myself. You are not a coward. And you have not deviated from the party line. Secondly, Sergo, I am a Georgian. And a Georgian must attract attention by his deeds. They used to say in Rome that the people need bread and circuses. There is one more reason as well."

"And what is that?"

Stalin began to recall one of the episodes from the revolution. The event had happened in Tiflis, the capital of Georgia when the underground Bolshevik organization had been mapping out an armed attack on the local arsenal. The question of weapons was then crucial. Lenin insisted on arming the proletariat. Some forty people were involved. Sergo was the head of the main squad, and Stalin was the liaison with the center. The plan had been worked out in detail two weeks in advance. But on the evening of the attack, seven people, in addition to Sergo, were arrested by czarist gendarmes. Sergo spent two and a half years in jail, and then escaped. Some questions remained: How did the police know about the attack and where the participants lived? Who gave them away? Even the Central Committee of the party had become involved in these questions. The investigation had brought no results.

"Do you want me to divulge the secret, Sergo? Do you want to know who turned you over?"

"Who?"

"I did," Stalin said, very quietly.

"You're joking." Sergo laughed.

"No, no, I am not." Stalin laughed, too.

"Stop, please, what a time for such foolishness."

"It is not foolishness," Stalin said seriously. "It is the truth. Please allow me to explain some of the circumstances."

"I don't want to listen."

"Sergo, we are revolutionary friends, but I am still the secretary general of the Central Committee, and tomorrow you will be only a deputy minister. You must respect rank. Be patient and listen to what I have to tell you.

"You see, Sergo, for three years I was a secret agent for the czarist police. When I was co-opted into the Central Committee, I broke with the police. Nevertheless, for three years—yes, three years—I worked for the czar. During that time I had to inform on those involved in the proposed attack on the arsenal. I had to divulge other information, but that did not concern you."

"I don't understand, Koba, why you've decided to play this trick on me."

"Don't worry. We are grown-up people, and we are

comrades in arms. Students of Lenin. Hear me out. So . . .
It should not be difficult to understand that during the first
years of the Soviet regime, until Stalin became great, I was
afraid that my secret would get out. But now that I *am* great,
none of this makes any difference."

"You've lost your mind!"

"Don't interrupt Comrade Stalin! Now you could go to
Red Square, up to the platform of the Lenin Mausoleum and
shout out that Stalin was an agent in the czarist secret police
and nothing would happen. No one would believe this even
in the capitalist West. Even if they did, it wouldn't change
anything. By the way, I understand that Napoleon Bonaparte started out as an informant."

Sergo jumped up from the couch and began running
around the room.

"Be serious, Koba," Sergo implored. "Think of what
you're saying."

But Stalin was obviously getting pleasure from Sergo's
confusion.

"What is so reprehensible?" he asked. "We government
rulers need such experience; it brings us wisdom. You consider me a cynic? On the contrary. Two questions arise
here, Sergo. First, did the czarist gendarmes later try to
blackmail me? Yes, they did. But I was underground and
that complicated their job. When I was arrested, I promised
to give them information again. But I fooled them. The second question: Why am I telling you all this?"

"Why?"

"You see, my friend, this is a deeply psychological matter. How can I explain it to you. If a person keeps a secret
for a long time, then it becomes a burden. I wanted to tell
someone, and you were my first victim, I mean you were

the first person I informed on. Aside from that, Sergo, perhaps I like to test my greatness. I can allow myself the luxury, you see, of telling you that I, the great Stalin, was an agent in the czarist secret police. No one else would dare say such a thing, but I can. Do you understand?''

''No!''

''Ah, you . . . well, probably, only someone of equal caliber could understand this.''

''Ambition?'' Sergo asked.

''To some extent, yes. Ambition, but not so much personal as political ambition. I revel in the greatness and the flexibility of Lenin's ideas. Ha, ha, ha! To put it another way, these ideas are similar to those of the great Machiavelli. It seems to me he said: 'The end justifies the means.' '' Stalin smiled. ''Anyway, how are you feeling, my revolutionary friend?''

''You told me a lie about Comrade Stalin!''

''So that's how it is, you don't believe me?''

''No, I do not believe you, Koba.''

''You think that I am a liar?''

''Yes.''

''That is very interesting. Look at this daredevil! He's just returned from exile, and yet has the courage to call me a liar.''

''To me, Comrade Stalin is the ideal!'' Sergo declared proudly. ''The same ideal that Lenin was.''

''Do you really think that Lenin did not have sins?''

''Lenin and Stalin are ideals to me. I live and die by them!''

''Good fellow! What a good fellow! It's good just to look at you. Would that there were another like you. Here we have a real, unbending Bolshevik, a Leninist, a Stalinist!''

The leader scratched the right side of his mustache. "And so, Sergo, you don't believe me?"

"I do not believe you," Sergo answered stubbornly.

Stalin's voice became as cold as ice. "In that case, I will send you back to Stalin's corrective-labor camp, so that they can straighten out your brains. Now you will serve time for calling Stalin a liar."

"I am willing, Koba," Sergo said. "It was in labor camp that we organized the Communist party cell illegally. We were Bolsheviks even in camp. Yes, yes, Koba, and in camp we remained Leninists and Stalinists."

"Who is we?"

"We, the Bolsheviks."

"Very well, I won't contradict you. Go back to camp, join your cell again and study Marx's *Kapital*. I will send Sopha back to camp as well. This very minute. I'm not joking, Sergo. One or the other, take your pick. Either you believe Comrade Stalin, the living one who is standing in front of you, and not the icon, or back you go to the corrective-labor camp."

"I don't believe my ears."

"My hands do not tremble, Sergo, you know me."

"Koba!"

"Well, do you believe that Stalin was an agent in the czarist secret police or not?"

Sergo said softly:

"Why do you take away from me the last thing I lived for?"

"Faith?"

Sergo nodded and his shoulders quivered.

"For the last time, Sergo, do you believe me or not?"

"Why do you torture me, Koba?" Sergo whispered.

"Yes or no?"

Sergo lowered his head. "Yes, I believe you."

Immediately Stalin changed. The coldness in his voice disappeared, and a soft smile played about his lips. He put his hand on Sergo's shoulder and said in a friendly manner:

"Very well. You did the right thing. You chose the right answer. Otherwise, you would have seemed larger than life, like so many heroes of our plays and films, who are men of unflinching character, 100 percent patriotic, without the slightest weakness. We are all human beings, Sergo, human beings."

"How will I live now?" Sergo asked quietly.

"You will live magnificently, like all our ministers and their deputies. You will live in clover. Occasionally I will invite you to my *dacha* and occasionally we will reminisce about our revolutionary past. And I will tell you about my job in the czarist gendarmerie in greater detail."

Basketball

A meeting of the Politburo had been set for two o'clock in Stalin's office. All the members were in their seats ten minutes before the meeting. Stalin arrived exactly at two.

This was not the usual pattern, particularly since the Politburo had met infrequently over the last few years. The leader assembled his comrades and disciples only on special occasions, otherwise making all important decisions by himself. From time to time, he would consult with one or another of the members, informing them of his decisions after the fact. He had to do it this way, because each of his "foster children" on the Politburo headed—or was meant to head—a specific branch of the national economy, or a section of the government apparatus: public education, culture, sports, and so on. It was usually stated, for example, that Comrade Malenkov controlled the electric power stations, heavy industry, the secretariat of the Central Committee and the Ministry of Justice, but Comrade Kaganovich controlled, say, all forms of transportation, the Ministry of

Light Industry, and the Committee on Religious Affairs.

Naturally, the members of the Politburo who were gathered for the meeting felt as though this were their birthday because the mere fact that they were assembled meant that they were still indispensable. At the same time, they felt uneasy, because no one knew what the meeting would be about and Stalin loved surprises, never missing the chance to rake someone over the coals for this or the other failure at work, and giving one of his didactic lectures. That was the minimum they might expect.

Molotov, a man with a small chin and a jaundiced complexion, who wore glasses and whose mustache was completely yellowed from smoking, sat at the long table, which was covered with a blue cloth. His head was lowered and he bit his thin lips. He had a premonition that lightning would strike right over his head, because he had committed an offense, at least in the mind of the leader. Granted, there was an outside chance that Stalin would not bring up this particular matter. Beria and Malenkov, round-faced, with fingers that looked like sausages, were involved in a lively conversation. Beria was waving his hands around as usual. Voroshilov, now gray-haired, but once a brave cavalryman, was whistling something from *Carmen,* for he had been to this opera at the Bolshoi Theatre the night before. Kaganovich was, as always, biting his nails and scratching his bald head. Mikoyan, a man with black hair and a typically Armenian nose, was reading *Pravda,* probably for the second time.

The remaining members of the Politburo and the candidates (Stalin ordered Poskrebyshev to invite the candidates as well) sat almost motionless at the table and did not take their eyes off the entrance door.

As soon as Stalin appeared, there was total silence. The leader, slightly round-shouldered and wearing his military uniform, entered unhurriedly and said casually, without looking at those present:

"Good afternoon, comrades!"

Their answer resounded:

"Good afternoon, Josif Vissarionovich!"

Stalin was aware that he did not treat his comrades and disciples with high respect, but he could not help himself. He had been that way even with Winston Churchill at Teheran and Yalta. And it was noticeable. Stalin inwardly considered this one of the strongest Machiavellian weapons: Neglect subordinates.

Poskrebyshev accompanied the leader. At Stalin's desk he showed the leader some documents. The latter bent over and signed them. Poskrebyshev left. Stalin lit a cigarette, walked around the room and said:

"Well, comrades, let's start."

Malenkov, who also functioned as secretary, took up his pen. It was rumored that in his own office he liked to type with one finger. Stalin continued to walk around the office, stopping occasionally and scratching his mustache. He talked slowly, with his usual random pauses. His left arm was unnaturally close to his body and slightly raised.

The members and candidates of the Politburo sat in their seats and moved their heads like sunflowers turning to the light, afraid of losing the sun's rays.

"There is only one matter on our agenda today," Stalin began. "Basketball." He grinned, and with an ironic glance at Molotov, added: "Yes, yes, comrades, basketball. An innocent game, you might say. Perhaps some of these present, in fact, look on basketball as an entertaining sport. I do not. And it would be silly for me to explain to you, the rulers of the Soviet State, that basketball is, in fact, *big politics*. Let us not separate sports from politics, comrades."

Beria was the first to pick up the leader's train of thought. Gloating, he looked at Molotov. Yes, that Russian blockhead will get it today, thought Beria. This was very good, for Molotov had, on more than one occasion, gotten in the way of the marshal's influence on Stalin. The others also shifted their gaze to Molotov.

Meantime, Stalin continued.

"I repeat, sports are politics. Yes, and everything in our lives is subordinate to politics. This is what Marx and Lenin taught us, comrades. We cannot look at any problem independently of the party, without our preconceived party approach to that problem. And now, from a party point of view, how shall we evaluate the fact that at the European championship tournament in basketball, our combined Soviet team lost the final game? And to whom? France. Isn't that a political failure?"

Then Stalin added: "I trust, comrades, that you have read the newspapers and know what I am talking about. We lost to France. And this was a blow to socialism and a victory for capitalism, which still exists in France. Am I right, or am I not?"

"You are right, Comrade Stalin," came from all sides.

Molotov, already yellow, turned green; he even closed his eyes for a second or two. His premonition had turned out to be right. He knew Stalin too well to have expected mercy. Their talk about the loss of that game in Paris, during which Stalin had hit the table with his fist and called Molotov an ass, had left no hope.

Stalin continued:

"Basketball is the same kind of politics as football. Every sport becomes a political fact, particularly when we got out of the country. I should remind you, comrades, that three years ago Voroshilov, when he was in charge of sports, was strongly reproached when our football team lost to Yugoslavia. Is that not right, Kliment Efremovich?"

"Yes," Voroshilov said, a bit embarrassed. "The Yugoslavs kicked me in the ass!"

"Exactly." Stalin laughed.

Everyone laughed except Molotov.

"The Rusian people say: 'He who looks backward loses his eyes,' " Stalin remarked. "So, let us return to basketball. Let us listen to Comrade Molotov, who now controls our sports establishment. The following question will be directed at him. Explain to us, Comrade Molotov, what it is that happened."

Molotov opened up his notebook, took out a sheet of paper, licked his thin lips, and said in a dry wooden voice,

"I have already explained to you, Comrade Stalin . . ."

"No, not to me, explain to the members of the Politburo, Comrade Molotov. I do not rule the country alone, you know. May I ask, Comrade Molotov, who is to blame in this matter?"

"I am," Molotov said, "but I want to add to that . . ."

"What do you want to add?"

"The fact is, this was the first trip our team had made out of the country. We were not familiar with European basketball. It turns out that the French players were taller than 7 feet, 2 inches and even 7 feet, 4 inches. And ours were . . ."

"You picked out shorties." Stalin said sarcastically.

"No, not shorties, but we had only three players who were 7 feet, 2 inches."

"Would you look at him!" Stalin raised his voice. "In a

country of 200 million people, he could find only three who were 7 feet, 2 inches. You did not look very hard, Comrade Molotov. If you had looked seriously, you would have found players of 7 feet, 5 inches, dammit.''

''You are correct, Comrade Stalin,'' Molotov said. ''I accept the blame. I did not look hard enough. But we learn by our mistakes.''

''By our mistakes,'' Stalin repeated. ''What a convenient formula. Comrade Molotov, I am not convinced that the edge in basketball is decided by height alone. I think that shorties also can be effective if properly trained.''

''That is true, Comrade Stalin.'' Molotov's voice dropped.

''Let's see how our honored former basketball champion, Comrade Malenkov, looks at it.'' Stalin laughed.

''I was interested in sports in my youth, Josif Vissarionovich,'' Malenkov said.

To himself he thought that Stalin would undoubtedly take sports away from Molotov and give it to . . . whom?

At the same time Molotov felt that Stalin was softening a little.

''We were all interested in sports in our youth,'' the leader said. Turning to Molotov, he asked: ''What else can you tell the members of the Politburo?''

No, Stalin had not mellowed, and that meant that he, Molotov, would get the party's punishment, and that Stalin had decided on that before he told Poskrebyshev to call the meeting.

''It's very likely,'' said Molotov, ''that the climate had some effect. Paris was very cold and rainy.''

''The climate was unsuitable for our players,'' Stalin jeered. ''Perhaps they weren't dressed properly. And how about their food? Don't talk nonsense, Comrade Molotov. Soviet athletes must be the best in the world! They carry Marxist-Leninist ideas on their banners. To hell with the climate, Comrade Molotov!''

"To hell with the climate!" Beria echoed. "Our people should be the best even at the North Pole."

"Did you hear what Comrade Beria said, Comrade Molotov? Even at the North Pole."

"And I agree with that," Molotov said quickly.

The Politburo was silent.

"Useless chatter," Stalin said. "Time is precious. Let us summarize. Since this was the first time that our basketball team had played out of the country, I propose to reprimand Comrade Molotov and record this matter in his file. I trust, Comrade Molotov, that you will carry out your duties as minister of foreign affairs with more diligence."

Molotov swallowed this pill, relieved that the matter did not go beyond reprimand.

"Furthermore," Stalin continued, "I propose that the Soviet team be reorganized, and that a penalty be inflicted on each player, including the three who were 7 feet, 2 inches. Their salaries should be lowered. The coach should be expelled from the party, and the chairman of the Committee of Physical Culture should be severely reprimanded and given a last warning. Moreover, I want our state security to see if any ideological deviation was involved in this loss. Take care of that, Beria."

"Of course, Josif Vissarionovich," Beria said.

This was worse. Arrests and exile to corrective-labor camps could follow. It all began with the height of basketball players and ended with state security.

"Now the last point," Stalin said. "We will take the responsibility for sports away from Comrade Molotov, for he is overloaded, the poor man, and give them to . . . Comrade Mikoyan. He is a man of experience. I am sure that he will prove deserving of our trust. How is that? Anastas? Settled?''

Mikoyan had not expected such a turn of events, but he, of course, smiled and expressed his desire to control Soviet sports.

''First of all, Josif Vissarionovich, I will try to grow to 7 feet, 5 inches myself. And will make the others catch up,'' Mikoyan said jokingly.

''Excellent!'' said Stalin. ''I was always envious of tall people.''

Mikoyan sensed a reproach in these last words and was quick to correct himself:

''Height, Josif Vissarionovich, does not determine stature.''

The meeting of the Politburo had lasted no more than twenty minutes. Members and candidates were puzzled as they dispersed. Why had the leader summoned them? They asked the question, although they knew that sports, like everything else, was government business and that heads could fall over this matter. Besides, from time to time, Stalin needed to make a public whipping boy of one or another member of the Politburo.

And not one of them was immune to this.

Hamlet

Ambition was my ruin.

It is true that whenever I went to a restaurant and drank 600 grams of vodka, (Stolichnaya), I would turn red as a beet, perspire like a horse, get up from the table and loudly say—no, shout out—to everyone:

"All of you are shits, but I am Livanov!"

That was so. Fame had followed me around like a shadow since the day I played Soleni in Chekhov's *The Three Sisters* at the Moscow Art Theatre. The fact of the matter is that Stalin himself, yes, the great leader Stalin, came to the premiere. He was a theatergoer and particularly patronized the Moscow Art Theatre. And Stalin was very impressed by me. I was informed of this officially by our general manager, who in turn was informed by Stalin's close comrade, Zhdanov. Since then, I had been offered movie roles; I received high praises, awards, decorations; I appeared on radio and in concerts; I moved to a new apartment on Gorki Street.

I drank both before success and after success. As for shouting, "All of you are shits, but I am Livanov," I learned to do that only after fame had taken me under her wing, that is after *The Three Sisters* and, in fact, with Stalin's assistance.

No matter what you say, fame and success are necessary to an actor. They are lifelines. They open all the doors.

Here is an example. Since the days when I was in acting school, I dreamed of playing *Hamlet,* and of staging the play as well, because I was also a director. For some reason, however, *Hamlet* was relatively ignored in our socialistic country, and, what is worse, the Danish prince was considered a suspicious character, almost Nietzschean. In short, *Hamlet* was not in complete harmony with our great epoch. That was how they put it at the highest levels. *Hamlet* was therefore produced in our provincial theaters, and then only through the oversight of the local officials. Of course, when I first joined the Moscow Art Theatre, I was not able to convince the management to perform *Hamlet.* But after Stalin had honored me with his attention and after the theater critics of the leading newspapers praised me to the skies, I decided to act more decisively and to turn directly to the Central Committee of the Soviet Communist party.

Can you imagine that within a month the general manager called me and informed me that I could begin working on *Hamlet?* I practically kissed him and, in absentia, the party bureaucrat who lifted the ban for me and for the stage of the Moscow Art Theatre. Following that, I drank so much out of joy that my neighbors telephoned the militia. But it didn't go any further. I took hold of myself, forgot about the vodka, and settled down to collecting material. I spent whole days and even evenings in the Lenin library, reading everything that was ever written about *Hamlet,* although I was already familiar with all the theories of tragedy, and with all the criticism on the meaning of the play, and most important, on the character of Hamlet.

I started to work out my interpretation of the play, and to distribute the roles. I would, of course, play Hamlet, in the hope that I would thus fulfill my life's dream. *Hamlet* was already listed in the Moscow Art Theatre's repertoire of future productions.

Marvelous!

Then, during the course of those memorable and fervent days, I was invited to an official reception at the Kremlin. The occasion was the anniversary of the October Revolution. Could I refuse? What actor would refuse? This was a tremendous honor. For in the Georgievsky Hall the *crème de la crème* would assemble, the stars of our Soviet society, along with the leaders of the party and the government, which meant along with Comrade Stalin.

On the way to the reception, I decided to approach Stalin and discuss *Hamlet* with him. He would undoubtedly remember me. So I would just go up to him and say, "Hello, Comrade Stalin, I am Livanov." That's what I decided. But it was not quite so easy to carry out my plan. Georgievsky Hall was very crowded, a regular anthill. Our leaders, or rather our leader and his so-called brothers-in-arms, stood in a group in the corner and were of course surrounded by a tight circle of bodyguards, boys in blue suits with orange neckties. At the beginning, I didn't even recognize Stalin, for he is not noteworthy, of small height, with a small head, and somehow slightly crooked. But later I could distinguish him, particularly because the others stood away from him, even though they still formed an aureole around him. I approached the forbidden zone and tried to figure out how to attract the attention of our great leader.

While I was contemplating my plan of action, the leader himself noticed me. I am conspicuous and can be spotted a mile away. I am tall, broad-shouldered, and blessed with fine looks, I cannot deny that.

"Comrade Livanov!" he hailed me, taking three or four steps in my direction. "Come here."

I could not believe my ears. Stalin had hailed me, *me,* Livanov, and had remembered my name. The bodyguards, of course, stepped aside, and I was before the Great Helmsman, who very simply extended his hand to me, smiled and said:

"How are you, Comrade Livanov? I am happy to see you. How are you doing?"

No, I did not fall apart as one might expect, and I was not at a loss for words. On the contrary, I shook the leader's hand, perhaps too strongly, and said something like:

"Thank you, not too badly. I am working hard at the moment, Comrade Stalin."

"Aha, that is very good, Comrade Livanov," was the answer to that. "And what are you working on specifically, if I may ask?"

I realized that I had the opportunity to consult with Stalin about *Hamlet* and I enthusiastically started talking about my life's dream. I had to enlist Stalin's support in order to raise as much money for the production as would be necessary to have my ideas realized. I told Stalin how I saw the play, what I wanted to emphasize, what to de-emphasize, and so on, and so on.

Stalin listened attentively. I caught something lively, almost mischievous in his eyes, and this inspired me even more. I finished with the question:

"Josif Vissarionovich, what do you think of Shakespeare's *Hamlet?*"

(Oh, how I wanted to show everyone up and announce in some public place that I interpreted *Hamlet* according to the wishes of Comrade Stalin.)

"You see, Comrade Livanov," Stalin said, "I am not a specialist in Shakespeare [our leader was very modest]. And mainly, I do not like to impose my opinion on creative people."

"But," I interrupted Stalin, "you don't know how important it is for me to have your opinion."

"If you are asking for my advice, Comrade Livanov," said Stalin, "then perhaps I can give you that. Comrade Livanov, to the extent to which I understand Shakespeare's *Hamlet,* I see it as a product of petit-bourgeois imagination. You see, the idea of abstract honesty and absolute spiritual chastity are foreign to the Soviet man. What can he learn from *Hamlet?* Reflection? Neurasthenia? As a result, I do not understand why it is necessary for you to waste your enormous talent and our money on this medieval manifesto on individualism."

Something in me snapped. After that philosophical and intellectually irrefutable tirade, there was only one road open to me: to forget about *Hamlet* once and for all. I understood that I had made an irreparable mistake and had hung myself.

"That is, you consider . . ." I mumbled.

"No, no," Stalin said. "This is not an indictment. I am only giving advice. I am not, I repeat, *not,* a Shakespeare specialist. And my advice is not mandatory for you,

Comrade Livanov. You are an artist, and artists must be free as birds. You must follow your own inspirations.''

For a moment I thought he was ridiculing me, because in his eyes there was still something cheerful, even mischievous.

"You feel, nevertheless," I said, "that we should not perform *Hamlet* at the Moscow Art Theatre?"

"I am a party man and probably a dogmatist, Comrade Livanov," said Stalin. "Don't listen to me. Do your own job. The critics will decide who is right and who is not. We party men are oftentimes crusty."

Stalin said no more, and simply walked away from me in the direction of another celebrity who was eagerly wanting to pay his respects.

That was where my ambition took me.

What was there left for me after this? Should I follow Stalin's advice and abandon the idea of *Hamlet,* or should I follow Stalin's advice by ignoring his advice, in order to follow my own inspirations?

The leader had expressed his view very cleverly. He said that I was an artist and should be free as a bird. And he said that the critics would decide who is right and who is not.

Yes, except that I was a *Soviet* artist and could not deny that Stalin himself had spoken out quite decisively against *Hamlet* and had spoken out to me personally.

The following day, I gave notice to the general manager of our theater that I was resigning from *Hamlet* and then in the evening I went to a restaurant, drank 600 grams of vodka (Stolichnaya), turned red as a beet, perspired like a horse, got up from the table and loudly said—no, shouted out—to everyone:

"All of you are shits, but I am Livanov!"

Blue Sky

The day had not started well. Stalin was annoyed with his new boots; they squeaked like unoiled wagon wheels, although they looked fashionable, and in general Stalin liked them. Then came that stupid letter from the city fathers of Yoshar-Ola somewhere on the Volga River. They wanted Stalin's permission to name the newly built house of culture of the local meat-packing plant after his daughter, Svetlana. In addition, Poskrebyshev had decided not to answer these people himself, but to show the letter to the leader.

"Idiots," Stalin said, raising his voice. "Damn toadies! They'll be the end of me! Isn't it enough that in all Soviet novels the heroines are named Svetlana, and that in all Soviet movies there are also Svetlanas?"

He told Poskrebyshev to inform the city fathers that their request revolted Comrade Stalin.

It was not only the new boots or the naming of the meat-packing plant after Svetlana that had put Stalin off balance. Since the evening before he had been worried about the forthcoming meeting with an American correspondent to whom he had granted an interview. He wondered whatever had possessed him to agree. Ordinarily he declined such requests. He did not like to meet with foreigners and, besides, he knew that he had to weigh every word because that damned capitalist press tried always to present him in a bad light.

However, this American came through special channels, recommended by "our foreign friends."

Half an hour before the appointment, Marshal Beria arrived to brief Stalin on all the information state security had concerning Allan Brown.

"I must warn you, Josif Vissarionovich, batono," said Beria, "that the American is very tall, like a fire tower, and he speaks in a deep voice. He has a fantastic voice, like a wind instrument."

Stalin pursed his lips:

"And in general . . . is he normal?"

"Mentally? Completely normal," Beria answered, "and he laughs from morning till night. It's true, though, that he's a little deaf in his left ear."

"And does he have a hernia?" Stalin asked with a smirk. "Don't play the fool, Beria! I am interested in the political profile of this newsman. I couldn't care less about the size of his shoes."

Beria apologized and said that Allan Brown was from a wealthy Texas family. He had graduated from Princeton, had been a member of the Progressive party, from which he was later expelled, and had written a sensational book about the connection between American monopolies and German Fascists, in which he freely criticized the capitalist system.

"They really like to cut off the branch on which they are sitting," Stalin noted.

"But at the same time, Josif Vissarionovich, it is suspected that this Brown . . ."

"What? That he works for British intelligence?"

"No, for Japanese intelligence."

"That's strange," Stalin said. "Usually American liberals work for British intelligence."

"And moreover, Josif Vissarionovich, batono, it is suspected that this Brown has contact with . . ."

"Can't be with the Zionists. Is he a Jew?"

"No, but his grandfather David had a mistress: Rosa Bernstein. Originally she was from Berdichev and played the violin."

Stalin praised Beria for the fact that the Soviet State Security had been able to uncover Brown's past so thoroughly.

"And was he ever a member of the Ku-Klux-Klan?" asked Stalin.

"On this point my experts are in disagreement, Josif Vissarionovich, batono. Some say yes, some say no."

"Is he married?"

"He was divorced a year ago. His wife, Betty, was a movie star in Hollywood. She has enormous breasts. Size 40. But shortly after they were married, she became a Lesbian."

"Comrade Beria, I tell you sincerely that the leader of the international proletariat does not necessarily have to know all of these details. It is enough for me to know that capitalism is in a state of decay. But in what way is secondary. I must admit that I know very little about Lesbianism. Some time, during off-hours, you can explain to me what it is."

"With pleasure, Josif Vissarionovich," Beria said. "Anyway, this Brown is interested in women. He also drinks, drinks like a fish."

Beria added that Brown worked for the leading American

newspaper, the *New York Times,* made twenty thousand a year, owned a two-story house and three cars, a Ford, a Dodge, and a Citroën. He was also a member of the Society for the Prevention of Cruelty to Animals and of the Society of American Astrologers.

"His sign is Scorpio," said Beria.

"Astrology is a science for charlatans who try to cloud the minds of the working class," Stalin said. "They are slaves of imperialism, damn them! Tell me, Beria, does this Brown speak Russian?"

"He learned it especially for this meeting."

"Is that so? The idiot, it would have been better to learn Georgian." Stalin burst out laughing and pulled at his mustache.

Beria burst out laughing, too, and said:

"I am certain, Josif Vissarionovich, batono, that you will derive pleasure . . ."

Here Stalin interrupted.

"Comrade Stalin does not need pleasure," he said sternly. "If I have agreed to grant an interview with this American, it is only because he will be *politically* useful. Tell this Brown that Stalin usually refuses interviews with Western bourgeois correspondents. Tell him that I will spare ten minutes for him. And I think that during this interview it's better to remove my portrait from the wall. Let's have only Marx and Lenin."

"As you say, batono."

"Yes, remove my portrait."

Beria did so. Before he left, he told Stalin that Allan Brown's brother was a senator and a member of the Republican party. At the same time he controlled 40 percent of Hairshine, a large shampoo company.

Allan Brown arrived at exactly two o'clock. He waited ten minutes in the reception room for Stalin. He was indeed very tall and spoke Russian in a deep bass with a thick American accent. He was dressed in a plaid sports coat, narrow slacks, thick-soled shoes, and a tie with colorful roosters on it. Under his arm, he carried an elegant briefcase.

Beria took him informally by the arm and led him to Stalin.

"Mr. Brown, allow me to introduce Comrade Stalin!"

"Hello, Uncle Joe!" Brown said, cheerful and completely at ease.

To Beria's surprise, Stalin answered just as cheerfully, and with just as much ease:

"Hello, Yankee!"

Brown and Stalin burst out laughing. Beria joined them. Stalin got up from the table and extended his hand to Brown. Brown shook it warmly.

"Now that you're acquainted, I can leave you," Beria said, very pleased with such a successful beginning.

"One moment, Beria. Have you checked this gentleman's pockets? What if he brought an American bomb with him?"

Beria slapped Brown on the shoulder and said:

"What do you mean, Josif Vissarionovich, he's a nice fellow. We will give him one of our bombs when he returns to the USA so that he can blow capitalism to hell!"

"All right, all right, Beria, you're a little too witty."

When Beria had left, Stalin said:

"Sit down, Mr. Brown. Make yourself at home. You know that Comrade Stalin is a simple man and doesn't stand on ceremony. Comrade Stalin, when he meets people, never creates a distance between himself and others. So what shall we start with, Yankee? Only please try not to talk so loud, your voice is like a horn.''

''Oh, yes, of course,'' the American said, lowering his voice.

''And what shall we start with, Yankee?''

''I have a present for you.''

''What is it?''

Brown took a carefully wrapped package from his briefcase and gave it to Stalin.

''Shampoo?'' Stalin asked as he took the package.

''How did you know?''

''I know everything,'' Stalin answered. ''Hairshine. The best in the world. Right?''

''Right. The best in the world.'' The American seemed awed. ''By the way, your daughter, Svetlana, might like it.''

Stalin turned the bottle in his hands and then put it down on the table.

''Well then, thank you for the Hairshine.''

At this point the American was eager to begin.

''I have a thousand questions to ask,'' he said, ''and only ten minutes.''

''Consider that Comrade Stalin has given you fifteen minutes.''

The American quickly took off his sports coat and hung it on the back of the chair. Then he loosened his tie. Finally, with a clever movement of his feet, he slipped off his shoes. Stalin regarded Brown with some amazement.

''Are you ready, Uncle Joe?'' Brown asked as he sat down and put his feet on the conference table.

At this point Stalin took off his military tunic and hung it on the back of his chair. With a sigh of relief, he took off his new boots and sat next to the American, also putting his feet on the table.

"Go ahead, young man," said Stalin.

The interview began.

Stalin, who usually spoke relatively slowly, assumed— and even surpassed—the pace set by the Yankee. Brown recorded all the answers with lightning speed.

"First question: Do you believe in God?"

"I am an atheist."

"Do you believe in communism?"

"I am a Bolshevik."

"How much money do you have in Swiss banks?"

"Not a cent."

"Are you planning to export the Soviet system to the United States?"

"No."

"Why not?"

"Because you have your own people who will build their own Soviet system in the United States."

"Do you think we have such people?"

"Unquestionably, young man."

As Stalin talked, he observed how skillfully the American was writing down his answers.

"Do you have a mistress?" Brown asked.

"What?"

"A girlfriend?"

"I am an ascetic."

"Do you fish?"

"No."

"Hunt?"

"Sometimes."

"Are you the author of the Soviet constitution?"

"No."

"Then who wrote it?"

"The masses!"

The American applauded.

"Well put! You're a great guy!"

"Am I?"

"Whom do you love more, Marx or Lenin?"

"Both."

"Are you afraid of death?"

"No."

"Why not?"

"Because people throughout the world say Stalin is immortal."

"Congratulations, Uncle Joe," Brown said, "your answers are irrefutable. If only American presidents answered correspondents' questions the way you do. If only you would agree to be filmed in Hollywood."

"Let us continue, young man," Stalin said, with a smile. "You have enough eccentric characters in Hollywood."

"Very well," Brown said. "Do you have the atom bomb in the USSR?"

"Yes, yes, and again yes."

"And is it true that you stole the secret from the Americans?"

"If you are not caught, you are not a thief, say the Russian people." Stalin twirled his mustache. "But let me say that we have splendid scientists in our country."

"Who killed Trotsky?"

"Who is Trotsky?"

"Mm, mm." Brown apparently decided not to press this question further. "Is it true that there are fifteen million political prisoners in concentration camps?"

"We have no concentration camps in this country, young man."

"Is it true that you travel in any one of five American Packards with bulletproof glass?"

"In any one of *four*. Accuracy is essential in these matters."

"Is it true that you have a manikin of Stalin that sits next to the chauffeur in the first Packard?"

"Old wives' tales."

"Between you and me, Uncle Joe, why don't you order a wax figure of Stalin from London? Madame Tussaud can make one so the masses will think it's the leader himself."

"Thank you for the advice."

Brown shifted his postion and stretched his legs.

"You're absolutely tireless, Uncle Joe. Here I am in a sweat. How about a short break?"

"Of course. If you would like, here is some Borzhomi mineral water, very good for you."

"Oh yes, I have heard of it. Stalin's Borzhomi."

Brown reached for the bottle of Borzhomi, which stood on the conference table, opened it, and started to drink straight from the bottle. Stalin stood up and walked around the office in his stocking feet, then stopped before Brown to ask:

"Did you study stenography in college?"

"Oh, yes."

"Splendid. It was not in vain that Comrade Stalin once said that Yankees are industrious people. I was watching you: one move of the wrist and a hundred words on paper. Right?"

"I have a special method. One move of the wrist and a thousand words on paper."

The interview continued, and Brown asked: "What is

'democratic centralism'?''

Stalin, with his feet once more on the table, smiled and said:

"If we are to believe our enemies, then 'democratic centralism' in the USSR is when everyone together says yes, and everyone separately says no."

Brown burst out laughing.

"Do you consider yourself a Russian monarch?"

"No."

"Why not?"

"Because I am the *red* monarch," Stalin answered jokingly.

"Well done, what an answer!"

Brown laughed again and asked:

"Do you infiltrate spies into America?"

"Sometimes, young man. In our era not one government can get along without spies. This is an era of spies, alas."

"Is it true that at night you sit through two American westerns?"

"Sometimes, young man, even three."

"Is it true that Stalin is the Lenin of our day?"

"Yes."

"Why?"

Here Stalin became a bit angry. "What do you mean, why? He took over. Stalin carries on Lenin's work. That is why."

"Is there a gulf between you and the masses?"

"No, there is not," Stalin said emphatically. "Do not pass on imperialist ravings, young man! Stalin is the masses, and the masses are Stalin. Is that clear?"

"Is it true that the deputies of the Supreme Soviet are designated by you in advance?"

"Yes, that is, no, dammit!"

"Do you want to be buried in Moscow or in your native Georgia?"

"I am not sure that the Russian people will give my body to the Georgian people."

"Is it true that you call the members of your Politburo 'kittens'?"

This question served to relieve the tension that had been built up. Stalin hesitated, smiled warmly at Brown, and said:

"You are very well informed, young man. They are 'kittens.' I have no idea what they will do after I die."

"Tell me, Uncle Joe, is it true that you conducted the war relying only on a globe of the world?"

"For a brilliant commander in chief, that is sufficient."

"To win a war?"

"I did not win it."

"Then who did?"

"The Soviet people."

"O.K. Tell me, are you planning to send the Bolshoi Ballet to America?"

"The Bolshoi Ballet? Well, what of it, we probably will. Undoubtedly, in fact, young man."

"I apologize in advance for the following question, but I must ask it because I'm a Western correspondent."

"Go right ahead."

"Why do the Soviet people make a fetish out of Stalin?"

"Stalin is for them a symbol of victory and a happy future. This is a fetishism of ideas. That's all there is to it."

"I've been in Moscow for three days. Everyone I've met speaks of you as a god. In one apartment I saw your portrait in every room and there were four rooms. What's more, I found a bust of you in the bathroom."

"Is that so? Mm, that's something."

"Do you like that idea?"

"Not very much. The fact of the matter is that some so-called Stalinists are bad and harmful people. They try to hide their real selves behind Stalin's portraits and busts in their apartments and bathrooms. Do not jump to conclusions, Mr. Brown. But you must agree that I cannot forbid honest Soviet citizens from hanging my portrait on their walls. That is their right, their constitutional right."

The American then asked about the factory that manufactured the "colossal quantity" of Stalin's portraits, busts, and statues. "To think that all of the buildings in your country, even barbershops, are decorated with them," Brown said.

"There are many such factories," Stalin said, "not just one."

Brown called this big business, but Stalin corrected him and called it government business.

Then the American told an anecdote:

"Listen to this one, Uncle Joe. A Moscow Jew is reading *Pravda,* where it is written that the Soviet citizens will not only catch up to, but surpass America. The Jew then turns to his wife and says: 'Sarah, at the point we surpass America, we will get off and stay there.' "

When Stalin's amiable laughter seemed to be a sign of encouragement, the American told another anecdote:

"Before the Soviet people entered the new Communist era, Stalin decided that they must pass through mass floggings. And so he gave the order to the Central Committee. The following Sunday, millions of workers came to Red Square and chanted the slogan, 'From flogging to Communism!' "

Stalin frowned.

"You are a brave man, Mr. Brown. Not everyone would risk telling such an anecdote to the leader of the international proletariat."

"Yes, but I have an American passport," Brown said confidently.

"To a Bolshevik, that is a blank sheet of paper," Stalin said. "You can get to Siberia with it, too."

"Allow me to ask a final question, Uncle Joe. As the leader of the international proletariat, can you explain to me why the sky is blue?"

"Why the sky is blue?"

"Yes."

"Is it blue?"

"Look out the window. It is blue."

"Indeed," said Stalin, looking out the window. "It is blue."

"Why?" pressed the American. "Do you know?"

Stalin abruptly removed his feet from the table and stood up. He said in a metallic voice:

"Your time is up, Mr. Brown. The fifteen minutes I promised you are up."

"O.K. But there was one question you could not handle, Uncle Joe."

The American also got up from the table, put on his shoes, and then reached for his sports coat. Stalin bent to pick up his boots, and said:

"Allow me, young man, to give you a souvenir of our meeting. I know you Westerners love souvenirs. Here, take these boots to America. They are mine, brand new."

Brown wondered, had Stalin really given him his boots? He was ready to hug Stalin, but hesitated.

"Thank you, Uncle Joe, I will never forget you. I don't

know how to thank you.''

Beria entered the room. Before he had a chance to open his mouth, Stalin said:

"Comrade Beria, make sure that Mr. Brown has the opportunity to see everything in our country that he wants to see. He is a wonderful American.''

"Of course, Josif Vissarionovich, of course,'' Beria answered.

"Good-by, Yankee from Texas!'' Stalin extended his hand to the American.

The farewell handshake was a warm one.

After he had accompanied Allan Brown into the reception room, Beria returned to Stalin's office.

"Josif Vissarionovich, you gave him your new boots.''

"What of it?''

"He will make a million dollars on them. They are *Stalin's* boots.''

"So be it. I won't miss them. They squeaked too much anyway. And if he really works for Japanese intelligence, he could be very useful to us. Sit down, Beria.'' Stalin went over to his desk and sat down. "We need types like that with infantile brains. Astrologers, so to speak. Scorpions. Ha, ha, ha! Listen, Beria, send Brown to Georgia, let them give a lavish banquet in his honor, something Georgians know how to do well. Make sure he is served plenty of wine, and then have your people present him with a young lady, blond of course. Photograph him with her in an appropriate pose. And then recruit him in the United States. Let him work for Soviet intelligence.''

"Perfect, Josif Vissarionovich.''

"And yes, Beria. Hang my portrait in place.''

Beria took the portrait of Stalin and hung it in its usual place.

Stalin got up from his desk and went to the conference table. Sitting in the chair in which Brown had sat, he put his feet up on the conference table.

"Beria," he said, "isn't it high time to teach stenography in our schools? One twist of the wrist and a thousand words on paper. A miracle. Tell this to the minister of education. It's high time."

"High time, Josif Vissarionovich, I will tell him."

"Another thing, that Texan gave me a good idea. A wax figure of Stalin must be ordered from London. The one we have now is made of papier-mâché. Why not have a wax one? It is more practical, Beria."

"We will order it, batono."

"One more thing. This American told me two anti-Soviet anecdotes. He picked them up in Moscow. Trace the sources. Punish the guilty accordingly. You know I don't like anecdotes. He visited someone in Moscow and uncovered four portraits of Comrade Stalin and a bust of Comrade Stalin in the bathroom. Do you know what that means?"

"Is that good . . . or bad?"

"That is counterrevolutionary, Comrade Beria! Such acts of sabotage and subversive behavior must be nipped in the bud."

"I agree, Josif Vissarionovich."

Beria started to put his own feet on the conference table, but Stalin quickly remonstrated:

"That which is permitted to the leader of the international proletariat and to his guests, especially foreign ones, is not permitted to Marshal Beria."

"Forgive me, batono."

"Beria, call the president of the Academy of Sciences of the USSR and find out for me personally why the sky is blue. I want to know why the sky is blue.''

"That is a very interesting question," Beria remarked. "I had never thought about it. Really, why is the sky blue? Why not green or yellow?"

"Exactly."

"We still know so little about life, batono."

"You may know little, Beria, but I know a great deal. It's just that I don't know why the sky is blue. I am puzzled by that. Listen, Beria, tell the guards to have my old boots sent to me from my *dacha*."

"It will be done."

Suddenly Stalin began to shout in a fury:

"How did that long-legged American find out that we have fifteen million political prisoners in concentration camps? Who told him these secrets?"

"I have no idea, Josif Vissarionovich," Beria said submissively.

"Another leak of our statistics, dammit! Check all channels, Beria! The offender must be shot. Fifteen million! That is an accurate number. The American could not have made it up."

"Yes, Comrade Stalin!"

Stalin pointed to the conference table. "The Yankee presented me with that package of Hairshine shampoo. The best in the world. Send it to Svetlana. Perhaps she will be pleased with this American nonsense."

"It will be sent, Josif Vissarionovich."

"That is all. You may go."

"You didn't tell me when you would like me to explain about Lesbianism."

"Later, later, I am busy now. This Texan gave me one more idea. We must send the Bolshoi Ballet to the United

States. Consider all the necessary aspects.''

Beria left Stalin's office with the bottle of shampoo. Stalin went to the window, shook his head and said aloud:

"Why is this damned sky blue? Why? Why?''

The Bolshevik Landlord

Stalin had a friend, Vano Sturua, who had been a fellow fighter during the Revolution. He was a Georgian and a well-known expropriator, terrorist, Bolshevik, and Leninist. After the death of Vano, during the first years of the Soviet regime, many poems and books were written about him, plays about him were produced, and movies of him were made. There was even a ballet based on the life of Vano Sturua. And, of course, sculptors turned out not a few busts and monuments. That was because Vano had died untainted; that is to say, he was a pure revolutionary.

Things turned out differently for his brother, Georgi, who had also been involved in the revolutionary movement in Georgia, but always played a secondary role to that of his brother. He was a tall, handsome man, with an aquiline nose and thick unmanageable hair. With the help of his brother's fame, and also on his own merits, Georgi attained the position of chairman of the Presidium of the Supreme Soviet of the Georgian Republic and was, consequently, a deputy chairman of the Presidium of the Supreme Soviet of the USSR. In other countries this would have corresponded to being president, but in the USSR he was merely a dummy figure, even though the chairman of the Presidium of the Supreme Soviet of any Soviet republic is automatically a member of the Central Committee of the Communist party of that republic, and that carries a certain amount of weight.

Anyway, Georgi was a bigwig and lived in style, with a luxury, government-sponsored *dacha* in Tskhnety, on the outskirts of Tbilisi, and two apartments, one in Tbilisi and one in Moscow. His *dacha* was an estate and it was this *dacha* that brought Georgi to the point of catastrophe. In fact, his estate became nothing short of a collective farm, except that the profits did not go to the farmers but into Georgi's own pocket. There were horse stables, cowsheds, gardens, seedbeds, chicken coops, and other things.

And so it happened that Georgi, the brother of Vano, became a kind of Soviet landlord without even being aware of it. He took advantage of his high position and used government money and materials for his own benefit. Whether by his command, with or without his knowledge, the estate of Tskhnety became an island of capitalism in the socialist sea of Soviet Georgia. It reached the point that Georgi Sturua's hangers-on, that is his helpers, administrators, guards and so on, began to sell Sturua's meat and produce at local Tibilisi collective market places—milk from Sturua's cows, lamb from Sturua's flocks, chickens from Sturua's chicken coops, and eggs, fruit and flowers from Sturua's estate. All of these products were of good quality, and still sold at a tolerable price.

Tbilisi housewives would get together and say things like:

"You know, Keto, today I made *kharcho* soup and my husband licked his plate clean. Why? Because I bought Sturua's lamb."

"You did the right thing, Nina. We drink milk only from Sturua's cows."

This was talked about openly, and no one thought anything of it.

But suddenly, like thunder rolling across a clear sky, an article was published in *Izvestia*. The affairs of the "swindlers" from Georgi Sturua's estate were discussed quite frankly. This was unheard of. How could a newspaper take a stand against the chairman of the Presidium of the Supreme Soviet of the Georgian Republic, without checking the facts and without consulting the chairman himself?

When Sturua read this article, his heart almost stopped. Immediately he concluded that this article would not have seen the light of day without Stalin's permission. Thank God, Georgi knew the mechanics of Soviet democracy. Yet this thought frightened him. In the beginning, he didn't even understand what the discussion was about: about his estate (what estate?); about his cows (what cows?); about his chickens (what chickens?). His way of life had become so habitual, he had become so accustomed to it all, that he had lost all objective sense of reality. His fear grew after the first Secretary of the Central Committee of the Communist party of Georgia called him and said that the article in *Izvestia* would be talked over at the bureau of the Central Committee. The voice of the first secretary was dry and official, even though he was aware that Vano Sturua had been Stalin's best friend and that Stalin had, as a result, always supported Georgi.

Georgi had to make a decisive move. His wife, an intelligent and well-educated Armenian, advised him to fly to Moscow and to see Stalin himself.

And Georgi flew to Moscow. As he sat in the airplane he thought of what awaited him. He realized that Stalin knew about his estate, that is, he had known about it before the *Izvestia* article. That meant either that someone had informed Stalin and Stalin had believed him, or Stalin had somehow investigated the matter through his own channels. Who could have informed him? Could it really have been Beria? No, Beria was on very good terms with Georgi, and Georgi often sent lambs, chicken, and all kinds of Georgian spices to Lavrenti in Moscow. Sometimes, Georgi had even sent something to Stalin.

"Whatever will be, will be, but I will go straight to Soso," Georgi decided.

As a member of the Central Committee of the Soviet Communist party, he was allowed to go into the Kremlin without a special pass and to enter Stalin's secretariat. As he waited for Poskrebyshev, Sturua understood that things were bad for him, having caught a mocking glance from one of the girls working in the office who had probably read the article and who probably recognized Sturua from photographs.

Poskrebyshev received Georgi about ten minutes later, which was perfectly normal. He rose a little from his chair as he always did at the sight of the chairman of the Presidium of the Supreme Soviet of the Georgian Republic, shook Sturua's hand and asked him to sit down.

"Comrade Poskrebyshev, I must see Comrade Stalin," Georgi said.

"Would you like me to report to him right now?" Poskrebyshev asked.

"Yes, if you would please. This is of great importance to me." There was a pleading smile on Georgi's lips.

He did not like Poskrebyshev; Poskrebyshev was too dry and impervious. For a Georgian, people like this were unacceptable. But he had no choice except to smile.

Poskrebyshev looked at his watch, and jerked his right ear lobe. Then he said:

"Very well, Comrade Sturua, I will try. We shall see what happens."

This gave Georgi some hope. Poskrebyshev, of course, knew about everything, but the fact that he spoke quite respectfully was a bit encouraging.

As Poskrebyshev entered the office, Stalin was sitting at his desk and busying himself with some papers. His face clearly reflected confusion, which very quickly turned into irritability. Poskrebyshev didn't have a chance to open his mouth before Stalin said:

"You cannot do this, Poskrebyshev. You've dumped everything in my lap. First of all, I am not a twenty-year-old boy. I am an old man. Secondly, I am opposed to such centralization. Others should do something as well. Must Comrade Stalin sign a statement of permission to establish a correspondent of *Pravda* in some Guinea? You cannot take one step without Stalin?"

"Josif Vissarionovich, as to the correspondent in Guinea, I informed you of that last week and you said that the matter should not be resolved without you."

"Very well, very well," Stalin said testily. "I am not reproaching you. I simply think that power should not be centralized in the hands of one person. Do you understand that? It is contrary to the teaching of Marx and Lenin. May I ask you, Comrade Poskrebyshev, what will you do after I die? I am not immortal you know. Well, all right, all right, what do you need me for?''

When Stalin heard the name Georgi Sturua, a frown appeared on the bridge of his nose and he squinted. He got up from his chair and walked around his office. As though he were talking to himself, he said:

"That means he flew in and wants to be received. He will try to explain to me that he isn't guilty. Or perhaps he will get down on his knees and beg me to forgive him." Stalin stopped in front of the window and looked out at the red flags swaying on the two spires of the GUM department store building on the other side of Red Square. "His brother Vano was a real Bolshevik, a Leninist. If Vano only knew what Georgi has become . . ."

The leader returned to his desk and sat down. "Poskrebyshev, tell this Sturua that Comrade Stalin does not deal with Bolshevik landlords."

With a nod of the head, Stalin dismissed Poskrebyshev.

Georgi Sturua's career was over. He called Beria, but the latter refused even to meet with him.

When Georgi returned to his *dacha* in Tskhnety, he said nothing to his wife, but went into his private room and unlocked his big safe. Vano's and Georgi's firearms were kept there. Both had had a weakness for revolvers since childhood and both had collected them throughout their lives. In the safe there were more than twenty revolvers and pistols of different makes. There were Mausers, Parabellums, Brownings, and Nagants, Shteers, Walters, Smith & Wessons, Colts, and tiny ladies' revolvers that could fit in the palm of the hand.

Georgi took out his favorite Mauser and decided to kill himself with it. He wrote a letter to Stalin and a letter to his wife, as well as letters to his grown sons, Melor and Davie.

No, Georgi Sturua did not shoot himself. He couldn't get up the courage. He died a natural death. He was stripped of his high posts, but received a personal pension and lived in a lavish apartment in Tbilisi and kept one in Moscow in which his sons, who were studying in the best learning institutions in the country, lived. Georgi was not even expelled from the Soviet Communist party, and his collection of revolvers and pistols were not confiscated.

Most probably, Stalin did all of this because of Vano.

But the farmers who live around Tskhnety still call the estate on which the new chairman of the Supreme Soviet of the Georgian Republic now lives "Sturua's estate."

Two Geniuses

Yes, it was the meeting of two geniuses, not a genius with a non-genius, but a genius with a genius. And this was, of course, absolutely unique.

Stalin had just turned seventy. On this occasion, which was celebrated by all "progressive" humanity, Mao Tse-tung flew to Moscow with his large retinue.

The meeting between Stalin and the Chinese leader took place at Kuntsevo, where a new floor with an enormous hall had been built for the occasion. Here the two geniuses were to shake hands.

It was winter and there was snow on the ground.

All the members of the Politburo awaited Mao Tse-tung in Kuntsevo. Lavrenti Beria led them this time. It was during the period when Beria had outdistanced Malenkov (not for long, it's true) and had subjugated all the other "kittens."

Mao was tall, meaty, with a wide face and high cheek-bones. He smiled continually but with reserve, and repeated the same sound "siiaaooo," which his undersized but quick interpreter, Comrade Lee, translated very accurately to be sure, but each time in a new way, that is, by adding new meanings to this sound. The Chinese language is an absolute wonder.

Both Mao and his interpreter were dressed in the same way, in dark gray jackets and wide pants. This was the party uniform (it resembled the one that Stalin instituted in the Soviet Union in the thirties), which emphasized the ascetic nature of a revolutionary.

After general greetings and comments, Beria suggested that the Chinese leader go to the second floor to meet Stalin. Beria and Comrade Lee were the only ones who accompanied him upstairs.

"It is winter outside, snow and frost." Beria was smiling and obsequious. "But it is warm inside. You will not be cold. Comrade Lee, would you translate that for Comrade Mao Tse-tung."

Lee got on his tiptoes in an effort to reach his leader's ear, and whispered something. Mao closed his eyes, threw back his head and uttered one word:

"Siiaaooo."

Lee translated in an inspired and absorbed way:

"Chairman Mao said that he is not afraid of snow and frost. Chairman Mao said that snow and frost are like the shadows of the sun and waters, like the reflection of winter stars in a spring stream, like wood and fire arguing with each other in a fireplace. Chairman Mao said that the four seasons are like seasons of a human life: birth, maturity, old age, and death."

Beria had not expected such a long and eloquent translation of "siiaaooo," but he did not contradict, and only nodded his head and said:

"Yes, yes, of course. Chairman Mao is right! I agree with him completely about fire and wood. Tell Chairman Mao that Comrade Stalin is awaiting him with great anticipation."

Lee again stood on his tiptoes and whispered into the ear of his leader, and in answer Mao again closed his eyes and said:

"Siiaaooo."

Lee started again:

"Chairman Mao said . . ."

"Wait a minute, Comrade Lee," Beria said, "he didn't say anything yet."

"Chairman Mao said," Lee went on, "that for his entire life he has dreamed of meeting Comrade Stalin. For him Stalin is like the sound of a horn with which a shepherd calls his flock, like a diamond, like a teacher, like a brother, like a friend, and, finally, like a signpost at the crossroads."

"What?" asked Beria, "A signpost?"

"Chairman Mao said that doctors had forbidden him to fly," Lee continued, "but that he disobeyed orders and flew to Moscow on a magic bird of Soviet production that reminded him of a mountain eagle sprinkled with silvery coins, into the red heart of world revolution to congratulate our luminary, Comrade Stalin, on his birthday."

"Very well put, Comrade Lee," commented Beria. "Both short and long at the same time, right? Thank you for the translation, Comrade Lee. Please sit down, Comrade Mao. Comrade Lee, would Comrade Mao like to sit? Is he warm enough? Is everything all right?"

Once more Lee whispered into his leader's ear. In answer Mao slowly nodded his head, expressing his general state of contentment, but he did this without enthusiasm, as though he were angry at something.

"Comrade Lee," said Beria, "tell Comrade Mao that I beg his forgiveness but I must go to Comrade Stalin and escort him here."

After Lee had whispered into Mao's ear, the latter uttered his strange, brief sound:

"Siiaaooo."

"Chairman Mao said—" began Lee.

"Yes, yes, I know," Beria interjected. "The sun, stars, a post at the crossroads, and so on."

Beria headed for the door and disappeared. Lee shrugged his shoulders and began examining the hall, relating what he saw to Mao. But the Chinese leader remained on the couch, where he sat with closed eyes and leaned his head back as though he did not care where he was.

In the next room, Stalin was preparing for the meeting with Mao. He was dressed in his famous militarylike tunic of the secretary general of the Central Committee of the Soviet Communist party with his trousers inside his boots. He was freshly shaven (he had shaved twice that day), and had had a haircut. The leader was pacing back and forth and cogitating about a very important matter: how to bring Mao under his influence. He knew that this would not be easy; differences had existed between the Soviet and Chinese Communist parties since the 1920s and China was not Poland or Bulgaria, which Stalin had brought under his control without much trouble.

Beria decided to tell Stalin of a minor embarrassment that had occurred.

"Josif Vissarionovich, batono," he said, "everything was done in strict accordance with the plan. I sent five generals to Novosibirsk. Yesterday, Comrade Mao's plane en route from Peking to Moscow landed in Novosibirsk. We presented Chairman Mao with a king's dinner, and then we took him to the Novosibirsk Opera and Ballet Theatre, where he was shown Glier's *The Red Poppy*."

"And so?" Stalin asked impatiently.

"Well, how can I put this, Josif Vissarionovich . . ." Beria adjusted the decorations on his marshal's uniform. "After the first act he got up and left. He did not like the ballet. My people telephoned me from Novosibirsk. They were in complete panic. The problem is, Josif Vissarionovich, batono, in *The Red Poppy* Soviet sailors fight with Chinese coolies on stage or something like that."

"Blockhead!"

"Who, Mao Tse-tung?"

"No, you, Beria!"

"But I was told that the action in *The Red Poppy* takes place in Chiang Kai-shek's time and not today in Communist China."

"What difference does it make?" Stalin was furious. "Did you do that on purpose? Who thought this up?"

Here Beria became confused.

"Excuse me, Josif Vissarionovich, but all this was your idea."

"My idea?"

"You ordered a stopover in Novosibirsk for a dinner in honor of the Chinese leader, and to take him to *The Red Poppy*. You had liked it. We rehearsed it for three months, spent a million rubles on the set."

"Don't talk nonsense, Beria!"

"Josif Vissarionovich, batono, I learned from several of Comrade Mao's people that he was enraged by *The Red Poppy* in Novosibirsk because he is writing a new poem that is also called *The Red Poppy*. You see, someone stole a title from someone."

"Rubbish!"

"I cross my heart, Josif Vissarionovich," Beria said. "You don't know what kind of person this is. He is a poet, he talks in images—nonstop, only in images—and images are often very hazy."

"That's not a problem. I can cope with images," Stalin said boldly.

"But it's my duty to warn you. And also, Josif Vissarionovich, we were not able to go through the contents of his pockets. He brought 140 bodyguards. A whole battalion. They absolutely refused to have a search. A shoot-out almost occurred between our people and his slanty-eyed ones."

"You are an idiot, Beria!" Stalin said angrily. "How dare you search Mao Tse-tung's pockets? How do you account for yourself? He has 800 million Chinese in his pockets. Speaking in images that is. Can you understand what that means? Beria, do you know who Comrade Mao Tse-tung is? He is the number-one person in the world . . . after me."

Stalin and Beria then went to the hall where Mao and his interpreter were. When Stalin entered he slowed his pace and approached the Chinese leader.

"Good day, Chairman Mao!"

Stalin extended his hand to Mao. The latter rose from the couch, also slowly. He smiled and shook Stalin's hand with restraint and dignity.

"Siiaaooo," was his pronouncement.

"Comrade Stalin, Chairman Mao said . . ."

Stalin ignored the interpreter:

"First I will speak," he said addressing the Chinese leader. "Chairman Mao, I extend to you an apology for the unforgivable incident that took place last night in Novosibirsk. It was, of course, an ideological blunder. Glier's ballet *The Red Poppy* is a vicious work, distorting and falsifying the historical and traditional relationship between Russia and China. The officials of the Committee on Art of the Soviet Union will be severely punished. I have already ordered that the choreographer of the theater and the soloist be fired and arrested. The question of Glier's work in general will be discussed at a special meeting of the Politburo of the Central Committee. Moreover, we will publish a party document in major newspapers to this effect."

The translation of Stalin's statement took some time. When Lee had finished whispering in Mao's ear, the latter produced a broad smile and this time cheerfully pronounced:

"Siiaaooo."

Lee promptly translated:

"Chairman Mao said that *The Red Poppy* is like a flower, a symbolic flower that expresses the image of the revolution, that poppies in the field are synonymous with crimson banners in the squares of London, Paris, and New York. Chairman Mao said that the history of red poppies is the history of the earth, the sky, crystals, water, light, moonlit clouds in the shape of elephants, the history of the origin of the first kiss between the wind and the fire in the universe."

Stalin kept nodding his head, and when the translation was finished he said:

"That is correct. I think, Comrade Chairman, that the subject matter in this case touches not only on the historical origin of the first kiss in the universe, but also on the first proletarian on earth. Is that not so?"

Lee whispered Stalin's words into Mao's ear and the latter closed his eyes and emitted his:

"Siiaaooo."

"Chairman Mao," Lee translated, "said that the questions of the dictatorship of the proletariat and of its leading role in the building of a socialist society are very clearly elucidated in the writings of the great Stalin, but that he, Comrade Mao, is trying to find a poetic interpretation of the combination of the red poppy and the poor Chinese peasant—or, to be more accurate, the peasant farm laborer—that is half proletarian."

"You must not make mistakes, Comrade Interpreter," Stalin said, "when you are translating the words of Chairman Mao."

"Please forgive me," said Lee. "Chairman Mao said that in the image of the red poppy emerges the velvet ocean at the hour of sunset, the gentle quivering of the bird of paradise, the peace and wisdom of the Himalayas at the hour of sunset, the glow of fire at the hour of sunset and the reflection of fear and joy in the eyes of a small Vietnamese woman . . ."

"At the hour of sunset," Stalin finished for Lee. Addressing himself to Beria, he lapsed into Georgian. "This Chinese leader is a blabbermouth. A poetic chatterbox."

Lee continued to translate the words of Mao.

"Chairman Mao said that the red poppy is the soul of a Japanese miner, the heart of a Filipino weaver, the conscience of an Indonesian fisherman, that it is a summons to the wind to become a revolutionary slogan so that it would be heard throughout the world, so that rivers would flow from the shores to drown out the fields of evil and oppression, so that mountains would move and crush the palaces of capitalism, so that a drop of dew, like a child's teardrop, like a mirror of beauty, would fall on the thousand-year wounds of the poor. Chairman Mao said that . . ."

"One moment, Comrade Interpreter," Stalin raised his right hand, "please take a short break."

Lee looked questioningly first at Stalin, then at Mao, who continued to stand in one place with his eyes closed. Stalin deliberately turned his back to the Chinese and began to speak to Beria in Georgian.

"I am sick and tired of this. Chairman Mao, Chairman Mao . . . Perhaps the Chinese leader is going to proclaim a cult to his own personality, a cult of the great, holy, infallible, and so forth. Yes? That would be a serious matter, Beria. The teachings of Marx, Engels, Lenin, and Stalin categorically renounce such cults. There is a definite danger hidden here. Right?"

"Without question," Beria answered. "Particularly since two great leaders cannot exist at the same time."

"Mm—yes, perhaps you are right. So what shall we do with this mandarin? First of all, let us shut the Chinese leader up. With presents. They say he likes presents."

Beria went into the next room to get the presents, while Stalin turned to face Mao.

"Comrade Chairman, I would like to honor this historic event, which will no doubt be recorded for all time by all peoples. I speak of your arrival in Moscow on the occasion of the seventieth birthday of our great, yes great, Stalin. In the name of our people, I would like to present you with a modest gift."

Beria returned with a black Caucasian mountaineer's dress, an Astrakhan hat and a dagger, and placed them on the couch.

"This is for you, Comrade Chairman. It is the costume of a toiling mountaineer, a Soviet mountaineer, the youngest brother of the great Russian people. I would like it, Comrade Chairman, if you would wear this costume and feel as happy in it as the toiling mountaineer of the great Soviet Union.''

Lee hurriedly translated all that for Mao, on his tiptoes and in his usual whisper. The Chinese leader again produced a broad grin and, throwing his head back in joy, emitted his sound:

"Siiaaooo.''

"Chairman Mao said,'' Lee translated, "that the toiling citizens of the great Soviet Union are the agents of progress throughout the world, that the Soviet citizen is the great giant holding the baton of the future in his hands, that he is . . .''

"A moonlit cloud in the shape of an elephant,'' Stalin interjected sarcastically. "That's enough. I understand. A translation is not needed.''

Lee became quiet. Mao clearly had his eye on the Caucasian dress, the Astrakhan hat, and the dagger. Beria took the initiative and proposed that Mao try on the Caucasian dress and the Astrakhan hat. The Chinese leader agreed immediately.

"Please, Comrade Chairman, here is the sleeve, like that . . . And here you must button it. And the belt, . . . that's right, like that . . . very good . . . and here are more buttons . . .'' Beria studied Mao, stepped back a step or two and proclaimed, "Splendid! As though it were tailored for you, Comrade Chairman. A real Abrek, even without a horse. Ha, ha.''

Mao answered automatically:

"Siiaaooo.''

Lee opened his mouth, but Stalin raised his right hand and stopped him, making it plain that everything was clear without his translation.

Stalin addressed Mao:

"Please pay particular attention to the adornments, Comrade Chairman. They are gold, yes, gold. And the dagger is a very expensive, unique work. The whole costume of a toiling Soviet mountaineer. That is, so to speak, a dialectical contradiction."

Stalin burst out laughing, but Lee quickly whispered something in the ear of the Chinese leader, who again brought forth his mysterious sound. Lee, quick as a bullet, translated so that Stalin would not interrupt him again.

"Chairman Mao said: Thank you."

"What? That was all? That short?" Beria was almost disappointed.

"Chairman Mao said no more," answered Lee.

Stalin coughed into his fist and remarked caustically to Beria in Georgian:

"There you go, and you said that the Chinese leader was a blabbermouth."

"Me? It was you, Josif Vissarionovich, who said that and not me."

By this time, Mao had decided to take the dagger out of the scabbard, but for some reason he could not do this despite all his efforts. Lee tried to help, but without success. The scabbard seemed to be soldered to the dagger or vice versa. Mao looked pleadingly at Stalin, but Stalin slowly shook his head to indicate to the Chinese that there was no point in even trying. Beria approached Mao and explained the problem.

"You see, Comrade Chairman, this dagger was sealed from the inside by the main office of the state security. We have a rule. That is, after all, a dangerous weapon. It is better not to tempt oneself. Comrade Lee, please translate what I have just said for Comrade Mao."

Lee whispered the translation of Beria's words into the

ear of the Chinese leader. Mao nodded his head in agreement. But then he emitted a particularly long sound.

"Siiaao-o-o-o-o-o-o-o-o-oooooooo!"

"Ah, ah, ah!" Beria gasped. "Now that is something special!

"Mm—yes," Stalin agreed, with some alarm.

Lee translated:

"Chairman Mao said that it is his turn now and that he would like to give to the great Stalin, in the name of our multimillion peoples, a present on the occasion of his seventieth birthday."

"It will be interesting to see what *they* thought up," Beria muttered to Stalin.

Mao nodded to Lee, and the interpreter, with a swift motion, removed a red Chinese robe embroidered with gold five-pointed stars from a small box he had brought with him. At this point, Mao again exclaimed:

"Siiaao-o-o-o-o-o-o-o-oooooooo!"

And Beria again gasped:

"Ah, ah, ah!"

Lee handed the robe to Stalin as he translated the Chinese leader's exclamation:

"Chairman Mao said that this is the costume of the toiling Chinese people in our country and he asks you, Comrade Stalin, to put it on and to feel as happy in it as each citizen of the great Chinese People's Republic!"

As Stalin took the robe from Lee, he said in an aside to Beria:

"Did you hear that? This Mao is imitating me, the son of a bitch. He repeats my words and he's a poet."

Beria, ever the obedient servant, began to pull the Chinese robe over Stalin saying:

"This is beautiful, what's true is true. What magnificent workmanship."

Mao again nodded to Lee, who took from the box a red Chinese hat with two long braids that hung to the ground. He gave the hat to Stalin and explained that he must put it on his head.

"Braids, no less . . . isn't that something!" Stalin laughed, but he still put the hat on his head.

"You look just like . . . like Confucius, Josif Vissarionovich," Beria cried as he threw up his hands.

Stalin brushed the marshal aside and said solemnly:

"Thank you very much, Comrade Chairman. This is a remarkable present. I couldn't think of a better one. I will cherish it until the last day of my life and will go to my grave in it, if, of course, my people permit me to. And now, Comrade Chairman, allow me to present you with an especially personal, I would even say intimate, gift. To the Marxist Mao Tse-tung from the Marxist Stalin."

Here the leader pointed to a box that lay on the round table and continued: "This is the historic address of Comrade Stalin on the subject of the Soviet Constitution, which has since acquired the name of Stalin's Constitution. This is a recording of the address. One hundred phonograph records. I hope that you will accept it."

Stalin lifted the box of records from the table, but he had not counted on the box being so heavy and almost dropped it. Beria quickly came to Stalin's aid.

"Dammit," Stalin swore angrily. "I didn't think it was so heavy." Then he noticed a sign on the box and became outraged: "Listen Beria, what did you write here? 'Breakable?' This is *breakable?*"

"Records, batono, Josif Vissarionovich, are fragile."

"Rubbish! They *cannot* be breakable. Stalin's address is recorded on them. Do you understand?"

"Precisely, Comrade Stalin," Beria's tone was military.

He bent over the box and in indelible ink added three letters, NON, before Breakable in large script. Lee whispered into Mao's ear during all this time, but the Chinese leader stood like a statue with his eyes closed.

Together Stalin and Beria lifted the box with the records and carried it to Mao. His eyes opened and a mixture of joy and fear played over his face as he took in the obvious weight of the box. He put one hand to his heart as though to complain of weak heart muscles, but then extended both arms and clasped the box to his chest. Immediately thereafter he handed over the box to Lee, who held it in his arms, swaying in such a way that his head could not be seen from behind the box.

As usual Mao said: "Siiaaooo."

The translation came from behind the box:

"Chairman Mao said that he will rise in the morning and immediately listen to these records, all one hundred of them. Chairman Mao said that he will repeat this procedure at bedtime. Chairman Mao said that he will do this instead of brushing his teeth . . ."

"What is this, mockery?" Stalin asked Beria in Georgian.

"How can you say that, batono. On the contrary," Beria answered also in Georgian, "this is the highest form of compliment. It is almost a heroic deed. The Chinese are very clean. They brush their teeth twice a day."

Mao again threw back his head and closed his eyes: "Siiaaooo."

Lee quickly lowered the records to the floor.

"Chairman Mao said that he, too, has a personal and intimate present for the great Stalin. To the Marxist Stalin from the Marxist Mao Tse-tung."

"This character certainly keeps up with me," Stalin said. "Let's see what else he's thought up."

At Mao's nod, Lee took a fan from the box and opened it up. This fan was red with a pattern of dots on it. Lee extended it to Stalin.

"It is now yours, Comrade Stalin," he said. "This is not simply a fan—*all* the writings of Mao Tse-tung are printed on it. And he has written a great deal."

"What?" Stalin cried, holding the fan in his hand.

"This is a rare work of art," Lee said. "A thousand Chinese specialists worked on this fan for a year and a half. You can read all the political and poetic compositions of Comrade Chairman through a magnifying glass."

"Fantastic!" Beria couldn't control himself. "I tell you, Josif Vissarionovich, they have outsmarted us, those damn Chinese." Then with enthusiasm he added, "What if we were to place all your writings, batono, on a . . . handkerchief, for example?"

"Idiot! Handkerchiefs are used to wipe noses. Don't you understand that?"

"Forgive me, I did not take that into account."

"Thank you very much, Comrade Chairman," Stalin said to Mao. "I value your political and poetic works highly. So far as the fan is concerned (Stalin fanned himself) may I say that such fans would be especially useful in hot, even stifling hot, capitalist countries. Is that not right, Comrade Chairman?"

After Lee had whispered into his ear, Mao burst out laughing, but with a delicate almost childlike laugh. He then uttered his mysterious sound, which Lee translated to mean:

"Stalin's humor is a biting *class* humor."

Stalin thanked him, of course.

The exchange of presents did not stop there. At the proper signal, Lee took a piece of ginseng from the box and handed it to Stalin on behalf of Mao:

"This is for Comrade Stalin so that he will live 1,000 years."

The Soviet leader took the root of life, smelled it, and gave it to Beria, grumbling:

"This must be examined thoroughly in the laboratory. I know these 1,000-year roots from which people end up in a horizontal position." In a loud voice he said to Mao: "I thank you for this as well, Comrade Chairman."

Mao would not retreat.

"Siiaaoooo," he said.

Lee began to translate:

"Comrade Chairman said that the root to life is located in the center of China, in the city of Peking, and in the center of the Soviet Union, in the city of Moscow. But that is not all. The root of life is located on the sun and on the moon. The root of life extends everywhere where there is air, a smile, and a kiss. The root of life makes white and black into red and navy, green and yellow. The root of life gives birth to both color and light. The root of life is the word, the song of the soul, the vibration of the string on a musical instrument. The root of life is everywhere . . ."

"He has gone crazy. Enough of this!" Stalin exclaimed in Georgian. "I am up to here with his stupid imagery."

"Be patient," Beria said. "You are a great person, but he is worth something too, you know, if he has 800 million Chinese in his pocket."

"You are right, Beria, we must be patient." Stalin was conciliatory now.

Lee droned on:

"Chairman Mao said that the root of life exists in every thought, in every misfortune of the worker, in every bead of perspiration on the forehead of the toiling peasant. The root of life . . ."

"I can't put up with this any longer!" Stalin exploded, "Enough! I understand. I understand everything without a translation. I would like, Comrade Chairman, to turn to the business part of our historic meeting. Let's consider that the ceremonial procedure is finished. Now, Comrade Chairman, I would like to discuss with you, without any witnesses, eye to eye as they say, the strategy and tactics of the Communist movement on a world-wide basis. What is your reaction to that, Comrade Chairman?"

Lee stretched upward and whispered into Mao's ear.

Beria switched to Georgian and shrugged his shoulders:

"Batono, Josif Vissarionovich, how will you discuss strategy and tactics with him? You don't know a word of Chinese, and he doesn't know a word of Russian or Georgian. In what language will you speak?"

"In the language of the revolution, Comrade Beria!" the leader answered. "In the language of the revolution!"

Mao's "siiaaooo" could be heard.

"See, Beria, I knew he would agree," Stalin said.

"Chairman Mao is in agreement with you, Comrade Stalin," Lee said.

"Wonderful!" exclaimed Stalin, "Very good! In that case, Comrade Beria, and you, Comrade Interpreter, need not be detained any longer. Thank you for your services. Next time, Comrade Interpreter, do not translate in the third person, translate in the first person. Stalin and Mao Tse-tung must be translated only in the first person. Without any of those 'he said that . . .' But you are still young and inexperienced. Are you a member of the Komsomol?''

"I am fifty years old," Lee said, obviously taken aback. "I am a member of the Communist party."

"You cannot tell the age of a Chinese, batono," Beria noted in Georgian. "They all appear to be Komsomol youths."

Mao pronounced his "siiaaooo."

Lee began his "Chairman Mao said that . . ."

But Stalin stopped him.

"No, no. That is not necessary. Comrade Chairman and I will come to an understanding by ourselves. You may go!"

"Yes, Josif Vissarionovich. I will in the meantime select a commission to draw up an official communiqué of your meeting. Whom would you like on the commission?"

"Malenkov and Pospelov," Stalin answered. "And don't forget to consult our Chinese comrades."

"Of course, of course, batono. Let us go, Comrade Lee."

Beria and Lee left the hall. Stalin and Mao smiled at each other, and looked at each other, not knowing what else to do. The dagger around Mao's waist and the tightly fitting Caucasian dress made it difficult for him to walk. The dagger slipped to the left, then to the right. Stalin had to think of the braids that dragged behind him on the floor, and on which he had almost stepped and fallen on two occasions. After some hesitation, Stalin indicated that they should take off their costumes. Mao readily agreed. Both sighed with relief when they were once again in their own clothes.

Approaching Mao, Stalin extended his hand. Mao again shook his hand. They even embraced and gave the appearance of kissing, although they were kissing the air. With a wide gesture, Stalin then suggested that they go to the center of one wall, where four portraits hung side by side: Marx, Lenin, Stalin, and Mao Tse-tung. Both men stood for a moment in front of the portraits in meditation and deep silence, as though they were paying tribute to the greats of this world. After this, Stalin, again by gestures, suggested a walk around the hall.

They walked from one end of the long hall to the other and back for approximately a half hour. They walked side by side, ceremoniously, trying not to collide. Stalin placed his right hand inside his tunic as Napoleon Bonaparte had, but Mao simply joined his hands over his big stomach. They stopped and smiled, of course, and Stalin twirled his mustache, while Mao blew his nose. They exchanged gestures that were unfamiliar to each other, and they both pretended to be thinking seriously. They again started to walk, and again stopped.

After that half hour of "exercise," Stalin escorted Mao to the table, on which several dozen eggs had been placed. He indicated that the eggs were nourishing, and, more important, safe to eat. Mao hesitated. Stalin then broke two eggs and swallowed their contents. Mao followed his example and took two eggs, but swallowed them whole in their shell, without breaking them. Stalin shrugged his shoulders in amazement. The Chinese leader let him know with a gesture that every nationality has its own customs.

Then they both sat down in upholstered chairs that swiveled. Stalin made a half-turn, Mao made two. His delicate but piercing laugh resounded. As a sign of solidarity, Stalin also laughed in a leisurely manner.

After they had exhausted their delight in playing carrousel, Stalin went to the special cabinet in which he kept his wines. He took out a bottle labeled Aleksandrauli and showed it to the Chinese leader. Mao rubbed the palms of his hands together in an expression of joy and energetically nodded his head. Stalin poured two glasses of wine and offered his Chinese counterpart his choice. Mao closed his eyes for a moment, opened them, counted something on his fingers, and then took the glass on the right. They raised their glasses, clicked them, and then drank, presumably to world revolution and global communism.

In a little while, they drank another glass, and then a third. Mao reached for a fourth glass, but Stalin intervened and suggested with a gesture that they compare their heights. Who was taller, that is to say. They stood back to back. Stalin raised himself slightly on his toes, but even so Mao was obviously taller. He indicated to Stalin, however, that Stalin was taller. Stalin shook his head. He considered truth to be the most important thing in life. He then sat the Chinese at the table and they began to compare strength, resting their elbows on the table and joining hands. Who would bend the arm of his opponent? They grunted, their faces reddened, perspiration poured from their foreheads. But it was a draw. Mao breathed heavily and put his left hand on his heart.

In an hour, when Beria entered the hall, he saw two geniuses sleeping in their easy chairs. Their heads had fallen slightly to one side. A rhythmic snore could be heard. The marshal could not immediately make out who was doing the snoring.

"Josif Vissarionovich . . ." Beria called out softly.

Stalin opened one eye and then the other, like a sheep dog. He got up, stretched, grunted, and then yawned.

"Oh, it's you, Beria . . . what do you want?" he asked.

"The Chinese is sound asleep, cannon fire couldn't wake
him. Well, is the communiqué ready?"

"Yes, batono, it turned out to be short, but I think con-
vincing and weighty."

"What you think concerns me very little, Comrade
Beria," Stalin said. "Where is it?"

"Here." Beria held out a sheet of paper.

"Very well, now read it to me, Beria."

"The beginning gives an account of Comrade Mao Tse-
tung's arrival in Moscow, the date, the time, and so forth.
Then it goes to your meeting today." Beria read the communiqué in a loud voice. "During the meeting of the two
leaders of the world proletariat and the toiling peasants,
Comrade Stalin and Comrade Mao Tse-tung . . ."

Stalin interrupted:

"Don't fly into a passion and don't raise your voice. The
chairman is still asleep. He should not be awakened. And
Mao Tse-tung's name should undoubtedly be mentioned
first. Then Stalin's. Is that clear?"

"Yes, Josif Vissarionovich," Beria answered, as he
thought to himself: "What a hypocrite!"

"Continue."

"Yes, batono. During the meeting of the two leaders of
the world proletariat and . . ."

"You have already read that!"

"Yes, yes, forgive me. Comrade Mao Tse-tung and
Comrade Stalin at Comrade Stalin's *dacha* . . ."

"Nonsense!" the leader said. "At the government
dacha, Beria, at the government *dacha*. Dammit! Comrade
Stalin does not have a *dacha* of his own. How many times
must I repeat that? Comrade Stalin has no personal belong-
ings. Why confuse world opinion?"

"Forgive me, batono—" Beria returned to the text of the

communiqué: "At the government *dacha* in Kuntsevo, questions relating to the tactics and strategy of the revolutionary movement on a global scale were discussed."

"The part about global scale is good. But the word strategy must come before tactics. Understood?"

"Yes, batono. The two leaders came to the conclusion that the concentration, consolidation and cooperation of the socialist forces in the world are increasing rapidly. The two leaders underlined the firm determination of the Soviet and Chinese peoples."

"Better say the Chinese and Soviet peoples," Stalin advised. "He is our guest. Mao Tse-tung. That means he should be given all the advantages. Why can't you understand that Beria? You're a Georgian."

"I did not write this document by myself, batono. Malenkov, Pospelov also worked . . ."

"All right, all right. They worked on it. Ha! The workers."

Beria continued to read:

"The two leaders underlined the firm determination of the Chinese and the Soviet peoples to help each other from now on, and always, and to strengthen their futures with the bonds of blood, spirit, and the teachings of Marx and Engels, Lenin, Stalin, and Mao Tse-tung."

At this point Stalin began to complain:

"There used to be four of us classics, now there are five, dammit! And a Chinese attached himself . . ."

"The two leaders," Beria went on, "pointed out the necessity for the strengthening, the sharpening, the reemphasis, the recharging, the rekindling, and the intensification of the ideological battle with capitalists of all colors and hues and with their lackeys of all colors and hues."

"Now that's very good. I like the word lackeys. Very good. Go on, Lavrenti Pavlovich."

"I inserted lackeys, batono. Malenkov was opposed to it."

"Is that so? I will keep that in mind . . ."

"The two leaders underlined, emphasized, announced, reported, and gave warning that the Union of Soviet Socialist Republics and the People's Republic of China will in the future lend full, diversified, multiformed, unlimited, and maximum support to the oppressed colonial and enslaved peoples of the world in their national fight for freedom."

"Right, Beria, right. Except at the beginning make the correction: the People's Republic of China and the Union of Soviet Socialist Republics. Not the other way around."

"I understand, Josif Vissarionovich. The two leaders charted a course in the creation of a great, a very great, a most great, a very most great society such as that in the Union of Soviet Socialist Republics and the People's Republic of China . . . forgive me, such as in the People's Republic of China and in the Union of Soviet Socialist Republics."

"Put 'most great' in bold face."

"Yes, batono," Beria said. "The two leaders announced that the triumph of communism on a world scale is inevitable, irrevocable, imminent, and that our children already live on the threshold of communism and are illuminated by its glow. That is all."

"As for glow, Malenkov probably put that in," Stalin said. "He is obsessed with 'glow.' But in this case it sounds poetic and corresponds to Mao Tse-tung's style. Very good. I congratulate you. You may pass the communiqué on to the world. Let the imperialists shake in their shoes. Inform our friends in the people's democracies and in the Communist parties in capitalist countries confidentially that Comrades Mao Tse-tung and Stalin will sleep tonight at the government *dacha*. No, add in the same room. And also add, in adjoining beds. Like that. Let everyone know that there are no disagreements between us.''

"Yes, yes, batono. May I go?"

"You may go, Beria."

"Forgive me, batono, but how about Mao? Do you think he will agree with the text of this document when he wakes up?"

"Siiaaooo," Stalin pronounced with a laugh and nodded his head.

At that precise moment Mao Tse-tung woke up, stretched, grunted, smiled good naturedly, began to look around, and then understood where he was. Having understood, he immediately felt his pockets to see if everything was in place.

"I greet you upon your waking up, Comrade Chairman," Stalin said smiling.

"How did you sleep, Comrade Chairman?" Beria asked.

Mao produced a broad smile and emitted his usual sound: "Siiaaooo."

Stalin said to Beria in Georgian:

"He still thinks he's God, the son of a bitch!"

Two Stalins

He walked around the table and checked the setting. A white napkin was wrapped around his hand as though he were a waiter in a restaurant. He was dressed in his generalissimo's tunic and his striped military pants were tucked into his boots. Time had taken its toll. Apparently unaware that he now slouched, he walked almost like an old man, not very confident or straight. But he was clean-shaven, his hair carefully combed. And he was in good spirits on this day.

The table was set for dinner. It was heaped with platters of Georgian appetizers—radishes, cucumbers, tomatoes, *tsitsmata,* a special herb, Georgian bread, fruit. There was wine and Borzhomi, by the goblet or even by the horn.

As he sang a Georgian song to himself, Stalin looked under the table to see how many bottles of wine were there. Rodionovna, an emaciated old woman with dark circles under her eyes, was at his side. She wore a long, old-fashioned Russian skirt, a blouse with an embroidered edge,

and felt boots. Stalin was accustomed to her and had entrusted her with the kitchen. He liked her for her unassuming manner, and for the fact that she was alone; her husband
and two grown sons had been killed during the war.

Now Stalin said to Rodionovna:

"Every Georgian, dear lady, is a born culinary specialist.
Do you know who goes to the market in the Georgian family? The husband."

"What does the wife do?" Once more Rodionovna
wiped off the plates, the knives, and the forks.

"She gossips. That's what Georgian women like to do."

"Our Russian woman would be glad to sit and cackle,
but she has no time. Too much work."

"Here in Moscow, dear lady, chickens are sold already
cut up. But in Georgia, they used to sell only *live* chickens.
They were cut up at home and cooked on the same day."

Rodionovna smacked her lips and said:

"You cut them up yourself, Sosiv Vissarinych."

"Cut who up, dear lady?" Stalin never bothered to correct her peasant pronunciation of his name.

"The chickens, the chickens." Then Rodionovna added,
"You take the chicken, spread it on the ground with its feet
in the air, and snap its neck with one hand. Then with an ordinary kitchen knife, the job is all done."

"No, it is not all done, dear Rodionovna. The chicken
has a heart, and even without a head, it flutters. Do you
know, when I was child I counted how long a chicken lives
without its head? From two to three minutes."

Boldly Rodionovna asked:

"Did you enjoy cutting them up or did you do it out of
necessity, Sosiv Vissarinych?"

"What do you mean, out of necessity?"

"Well, you don't trust anyone else. You don't even trust me. The other day when Beria wanted you to let him cut one up, you hushed him as though to say, 'how dare you!' "

"You're right, I hushed him up. I trust *you*, Rodionovna. Nevertheless, when it comes to chickens . . . I could say that I do it both out of love and out of necessity. I remember on the street where I lived in Gori, there also lived a man by the name of Serapion. He was a telegraph operator. But all his life, this Serapion cut up chickens for everyone on our street. Free of charge. Most probably he did it out of love. There was no necessity in it."

Rodionovna became very daring and decided to ask Stalin about a matter that had interested her for a long time.

"Sosiv Vissarinych, I know you are the son of a shoemaker, but someone told me that that is not so, and that you came from a family of princes? Is that true or not?"

"Who told you that, Rodionovna?"

"I would rather die than say who, because I swore to God I wouldn't."

"People say all kinds of things, Rodionovna. Is it worth believing them? With my hand on my heart I say to you, dear lady, I do not know myself whether it is true."

"How can that be?" Rodionovna started to blink rapidly.

Stalin smiled. "Dear lady, for a long time people have said that I come from a line of princes. Imagine this, Rodionovna. There once lived in Georgia a certain Prince Ignatashvili. And this prince spent the night, excuse the expression, with his serf girl, Keke. A boy, Soso, then appeared on this earth, the future leader of the international proletariat and of all 'progressive' humanity. The prince covered his sin, as the Russian people say, by giving Keke in marriage to a Gorian shoemaker, the drunkard Vissarion

Dzhugashvili. This devil, in accordance with the law of class hatred, began to beat little Soso because of his princely blood. You see my left arm is crippled. It was from that time."

"Then it is *true,* you do come from princes?"

"Perhaps it is true. Although they say this Ignatashvili was not a prince, but a priest."

"Then you come from priests?"

"I don't know, dear Rodionovna. God knows, I don't know. Perhaps from princes, perhaps from priests, perhaps from proletarians."

"The books say that you come from proletarians, but now you're saying . . . it looks like you're a bastard."

"Well, not quite."

"Who do you feel like?"

"That varies, Rodionovna."

"Sosiv Vissarinych, Beria calls you batono. You sometimes get angry, and at other times I have noticed it suits your heart. Why is that?"

"When I consider myself a prince, it suits my heart. When I consider myself a proletarian, I don't like it. Batono means master, Rodionovna, and almost all Georgians address each other as batono. But almost all Georgians, to this very day, consider themselves princes."

Here Stalin laughed.

"Sosiv Vissarinych," Rodionovna persisted, "if you are this prince, then why don't you live like a prince? Doesn't socialism allow for that? If not, let socialism go to the dogs. To tell the truth, you live just so-so! And you are the sovereign of all Russia."

"Oh, Rodionovna, how can a bastard become a sovereign?" Stalin asked jokingly.

"Why not throw a banquet for the whole world . . . eh?"

"A banquet? All right, let's have a banquet. But where will we find princes and princesses for our guests? Whom shall we invite to this banquet?"

"Your ministers, generals, and their wives, of course. Won't they be appropriate?"

"E-e-e-e, Rodionovna, what an idea! They're so cheap and money-conscious. I know who buys up all kinds of jewelry and valuables to hoard for a rainy day. If these people are fired from their positions, or if the Soviet regime ends, what will they do? No, Rodionovna, my ministers are parasites above all. They are companions to down vodka with. They get senselessly drunk, and then inevitably get into a bloody fight to prove that 'I'm not the thief, you're the thief.' No, dear lady, banquets are not for them. If only you could imagine how elegantly Georgian princes knew how to debauch in the past. They were aristocrats, Rodionovna, aristocrats."

"That is understandable, of course," said Rodionovna, although the word *aristocrat* was not familiar to her.

"By the way," Stalin said, "today I'm expecting a guest who is also an aristocrat. No, by God, not an aristocrat—he's from the aristocracy, to be more exact."

"Who is he? You certainly are putting yourself out for this honored guest."

"What's true is true, Rodionovna."

"Who are you expecting?"

"Can you guess? Name the very, very greatest."

"Could it be the patriarch of all Russia?"

"Higher."

"Higher? Who can be higher? Only God himself is higher."

"Don't be afraid to name him who is higher than God. Well?"

"There is no one!" Rodionovna exclaimed.

"Very well . . . next to God."

"Some apostle perhaps . . ."

At this moment, footsteps could be heard, and the door opened. In walked Beria in civilian dress, and after him came Mikhail Gelovani, the actor, in the uniform of the generalissimo of the USSR, made-up to look like Stalin. The resemblance was striking. Gelovani did seem a little taller than Stalin, and he held himself more erect, apparently trying to portray Stalin when he was young and handsome. And Gelovani's face bore no trace of smallpox. But he spoke with a Georgian accent, exactly like Stalin's, making long pauses at will, just as Stalin did. And his gestures were exactly like Stalin's.

"Hello, Comrade Stalin!" said Stalin.

"Oh Lord! Oh Lord! Oh Lord!" Rodionovna cried out in fright. She crossed herself and flew out of the dining room like a bullet.

"Hello, Comrade Stalin!" Stalin repeated with a laugh.

"Hello, Josif Vissarionovich!" Gelovani answered in a dignified manner.

They shook hands.

"Two Stalins. Now that's something," Beria said. "Good evening, Josif Vissarionovich, batono. Two Stalins! Now I am lost."

"You were lost with one Stalin, Beria." After this aside, Stalin addressed Gelovani: "I am pleased to meet you."

"I am happy, Josif Vissarionovich," Gelovani answered.

"Very, very pleased. We have met at last."

"Very, very pleased."

"No, no," Stalin noted jokingly, "do not imitate me word for word, please."

"No, no, of course not. Forgive me."

Beria again joined the conversation:

"I went in person to pick up Comrade Gelovani, Josif Vissarionovich. He lives in the house across from Mossovet's building in Gorki Street. And when Gelovani was getting into my car, the Soviet people saw him and began to applaud and shout, 'Long live the great Stalin!' "

"Is it permissible to ask if they slipped in a bomb?"

"Of course not, batono, they all know that Gelovani is the actor who portrays Stalin in the movies."

"I see, I see," Stalin said. "I think this is a rare, even unprecedented meeting. Is that not so? Who would doubt you look exactly like Comrade Stalin. Mikhail Georgievich, isn't it Mikhail Georgievich?" Gelovani nodded. "Now walk around the room, please."

The actor circled the room once. Stalin asked him to do this again.

"Excellent. Very good. You even walk like me. True, I walked like that when I was younger. Is it permissible to ask, Mikhail Georgievich, how many actors in our country play Comrade Stalin in the movies and theater? Or do you have the monopoly?"

"Well, Josif Vissarionovich, in the movies there are a few others. Depending on the occasion. I would say I'm a half-monopolist so far as the theater is concerned."

Beria interrupted Gelovani:

"You know, don't you, Josif Vissarionovich, batono, that in accordance with your order, every actor in the movies and theater has to be confirmed for the roles of

Comrades Lenin and Stalin by the special decision of the
Presidium of the Central Committee of the Soviet Communist party?''

"Oh yes, I forgot. That's right. Such an important matter
cannot be left unsupervised.''

Stalin took his cigarettes from his pocket and offered one
to Gelovani.

"Do you smoke?''

"Thank you. Only my own.'' And Gelovani took an
identical pack from his pocket.

"Look at him,'' Stalin said. "Even his cigarettes are like
Stalin's. Well, then, let's have a cigarette.''

They lighted their cigarettes and began to walk around
the dining room together. Beria, meantime, decided to "in-
spect'' the table and popped a radish in his mouth.

"All right, Comrade Gelovani,'' said Stalin, "I will
begin by noting that a serious burden falls on you. One
could even say an extremely serious burden. The Soviet
people—and peoples all over the world—want to know
what Stalin is like. It is your duty, Comrade Gelovani, to
show them Stalin, the way they have a right to see him.
And, moveover, you must create an authentic image of the
great Stalin so that he will be imprinted on the history of
mankind in an artistic mold that is distinct from, let's say, a
documentary film sequence.''

Stalin stopped in the middle of the room and was silent.
Gelovani also stopped. Beria, having swallowed the radish,
was thinking that the leader's lecture could take at least half
an hour and that he, Beria, very much wanted to eat.

"Now Mikhail Chiaurelli,'' Stalin continued, "our illus-
trious movie director, brings me his films. You know I like
Misha Chiaurelli and have befriended him. Yes, I watch his

films. I see all Soviet films and many foreign films. Let's take Chiaurelli's most recent work, *The Fall of Berlin*. This is an epoch-making film, and no doubt deserves a high rating. I have awarded the Stalin Prize to all of you who participated in the film. I hope you do not bear a grudge against me for that, Mikhail Georgievich.''

"How could you say that, Josif Vissarionovich," Gelovani hastened to say. "We are very grateful."

"Well, then. You play the role of Comrade Stalin as a brilliant commander and strategist. But tell me truthfully— your hand on your heart as the Russians say—did the brilliant commander and strategist really strike you as such a handsome fellow and such a . . . simpleton?''

Gelovani lowered his eyes and said quietly:

"Forgive me, Josif Vissarionovich, I was trying . . .''

"I understand that it was not your fault," the leader soothed him. "It was Chiaurelli who wanted Stalin still to be young. But is that right? Is it permissible to ask: Does this correspond to reality? No, it does not, and that is why it is not faithful from a political and an aesthetic point of view. Of course, Comrade Gelovani, my people want Stalin to live forever.''

Beria couldn't help sighing at this point.

"Beria, of course, does not count. He sighs, you see . . .''

As Beria began to protest, Stalin said: "Yes, my people want to see Stalin always young. However, youth is one thing and simple-mindedness is another, although there *is* a slight logical connection. Don't you think so, Mikhail Georgievich?'' Without waiting for an answer Stalin went on: "My dear comrades, all of this is of greater significance than you think. The Soviet people deserve to be told the truth, the truth, and once again, the truth. You, Comrade Gelovani, must . . . it is your responsibility to convey to our people, to our Soviet people, to the ordinary working men of the city and the village, the characteristic, the typical traits of Comrade Stalin, not forgetting, of course, the passage of time, which inevitably determines the historically concrete image of Stalin. Is that clear? But I do not think that simple-mindedness was at any time typical of Stalin's nature. Right, Comrade Beria?''

"That is right, Josif Vissarionovich!" Beria asserted.

Stalin began to circle the dining room alone, in deep thought. Beria unobtrusively signaled to Gelovani to bear up, as though to say that the old man had lost his senses but there was no other way out of the situation. Gelovani stood respectfully and followed the leader with his eyes.

Stalin then said:

"You know, I am against all those sugary scenes in which Lenin and Stalin kiss children and give them candy. I am against the scenes in which they sit in the kitchens of revolutionary workers and drink tea with them. It could get to the point where Lenin and Stalin, excuse me for saying this, suffer from indigestion on the stage or on the screen. Who is interested in that? Allow me to ask, who? The masses, the people? And who will believe it? No, no, and once again, no. Comrades Lenin and Stalin must be represented as titans of thought, wise men, philosophers, leaders of the world proletariat, as men of international dimension, as men who have changed the face of the world!''

"The physiognomy," Beria remarked.

"What? All right, have it your way, Beria, the physiognomy of the world—not face, but physiognomy. Now come with me, Mikhail Georgievich, I want to show you a few things.''

Stalin let Gelovani into his library on the first floor, and pointed to several book shelves.

"All these are collections of the works of the great Stalin. Do you know, Comrade Gelovani, how many copies of Comrade Stalin's works have been published in Russian and in other languages of the world? Seven hundred million in all. Yes, yes, seven hundred million. Even Leo Tolstoi cannot claim that many copies.

"Comrade Stalin is an old man. He is over seventy. But, nevertheless, Mikhail Georgievich, history still listens to him. He still, to a large extent, imposes on history the progressive tendencies in both economic and ideological spheres. I can give you a concrete example. But for that we must go into my study."

Stalin called Beria and headed toward his working room. Gelovani followed. On the leader's desk, among the papers, lay a thick notebook containing a new manuscript.

"Sit down, Mikhail Georgievich, here in the chair. And you, here, Beria."

Stalin picked up the thick notebook, opened it, and said:

"Now then, comrades, only yesterday I completed a new scientific work, *The Theory of Superstructural Categories*. In essence, it is a continuation of my classic work, *Marxism and the Question of Languages*, which I trust you have read, Mikhail Georgievich. Is that right?"

"Of course, of course," Gelovani answered quickly.

"Very good. In this scientific work, I show how Marr, the world-famous linguist and Soviet academician, while attributing to language a class meaning, or to be more exact, *only* a class meaning, ended up vulgarizing and simplifying Marxism as a whole. I will read you the work. In a few days, it will be accessible to millions. Here are only 100 pages . . ."

Stalin sat back in his chair and began to read. He read for more than three hours, slowly, making arbitrary pauses or stopping to twirl his mustache. It was very tedious and hard to understand, but Gelovani, for those entire three hours, did not take his eyes off the leader, trying to catch each of his intonations, all that was characteristic of Stalin. Beria signaled to Gelovani, well, we are lost, then he put his head in his hand and settled down. After he completed his reading, Stalin paused and asked Gelovani:

"Well?"

"Very, very interesting," he answered.

Beria jumped up and cried out:

"That was brilliant, Comrade Stalin! It opens a new door to science and philosophy. Scholars all over the world will now begin to rethink!"

"Of course they will rethink," Stalin said. "And next time, Comrade Beria, do not sleep when Stalin is reading his works."

"Who slept? I slept? How can you say that, batono? I remember every word. I can repeat it by heart, if you like."

"No need," Stalin said sarcastically.

"I would have this Marr shot. And tomorrow," Beria said decisively.

"You are too late," said Stalin. "He is already dead, and can you imagine he died without anyone's help, back in 1934."

"Well, then . . . then, Josif Vissarionovich, let's rename Marr Street in Tbilisi. It is a wide street, with many centers of higher learning, including the University of Soviet Georgia. What a disgrace! How could it bear the name of a vulgarizer of Marxism?"

". . . You are probably right, Beria," Stalin said, considering. "Sometimes you say things that are not so stupid. It would really not be a bad idea to rename Marr Street. We could name it Mikhail Gelovani Street, for example."

"Oh no, no," Gelovani cried out in fear, "such a street already exists, batono."

"How? Where?"

"Comrade Beria gave the order last year. I have a small house in Sukhumi. I bought it with honestly earned money. It is like a *dacha*. So the street on which this house stands is already called by the name of Mikhail Gelovani."

"So that's it." Stalin burst out laughing, and then said half seriously, half jokingly: "However, isn't it strange that we Bolsheviks, Marxists, Leninists, Stalinists name only collective farms, plants, streets, squares, and cities in honor of our outstanding people? Why not name rivers and seas after them? For example, instead of the Volga River, Molotov River; instead of the Caspian Sea, Lavrenti Beria Sea."

The marshal was much taken with this idea.

"And why not name the Atlantic Ocean the Stalin Ocean!" he exclaimed. "Would that be bad?"

"Bad," said Stalin. "I would still prefer to have the Pacific Ocean the Stalin Ocean."

"As you please, batono. It is up to you. If you want it to be the Pacific, then choose the Pacific. And if you like, it can be both. The Atlantic and the Pacific. Or we can take all the oceans and call them Stalin's oceans."

After a pause, Stalin said:

"Let us return to the image of Comrade Stalin, Mikhail Georgievich. I did not read my work on Marr without good reason. I wanted to acquaint you with a certain Comrade Stalin—a thinker, a philosopher, a philologist, an expert in aesthetics. In a word, a Comrade Stalin with whom you were acquainted but whom you have not brought to life. It is precisely this universal—I emphasize universal—Stalin whom it is necessary to bring to the consciousness of the people of our planet. Today, Mikhail Georgievich, you were given the opportunity to observe Stalin more closely. But keep in mind that while this will alleviate your burden, it will also place a great responsibility on your shoulders. Until now you could say, 'What do you want from me, I have never even seen Stalin.' Tomorrow you can no longer say that. So I urge you, show our great Stalin in greater depth and seriousness. And don't forget that personality still has a certain significance in history. Do you understand me, Mikhail Georgievich?''

Gelovani rose from his chair.

"Yes, yes, I will try. I will exert every effort."

"Think. Concentrate your thoughts. On the screen, in the theater, in novels, Stalin must always be thinking, concentrating. For essentially the thoughts of Stalin are the thoughts of the entire people, of all progressive humanity, if you like."

Beria could not help blurting out:

"Josif Vissarionovich, the Russian people say: 'You cannot feed a nightingale with a fairy tale.' Gelovani is probably hungry, eh?"

Stalin continued to address Gelovani:

"And now for the 'screen Stalin.' In outward appearance I think you have approximated me. More closely I think than any of the other Soviet actors. But, of course, the fact that you are Georgian helped you. What can I say? We Bolsheviks are a modest people, that is a well-known fact. We talk little of ourselves. If I talked to you about Stalin, that does not mean that I was talking about myself. I hope you understand me. Well then, I would take his good looks away from your Stalin. They are not important. Frankly, I was never handsome. How can a person be handsome if his face is pockmarked? In addition, you raise your left arm too much. Now please observe how I raise it.'' After Stalin had demonstrated this to Gelovani, he added: ''Let's see you do that.''

Obviously feeling awkward, Gelovani stepped to the middle of the room and showed how he could raise his left arm. Stalin observed him, and made comparisons with his own left hand.

''What do you think, Comrade Beria?''

''A little too high. I say Gelovani raises it a little too high. You are right, batono.''

''It looks a bit exaggerated, Mikhail Georgievich. And your step, your step is longer than mine. Watch how I walk.'' Stalin walked around his study. ''Notice that I drop a little between steps, but do not swing my shoulders. Watch again. Did you notice?''

''Yes, Josif Vissarionovich. I understand what you are saying.'' Gelovani tried very hard to copy Stalin's walk. ''I will work on it.''

''Well, now, one more time, one more time . . .'' and in reaction to Gelovani's new efforts, Stalin commented: ''Better this time, I think. What do you think, Lavrenti Pavlovich?''

''I think, yes and no.''

''What do you mean, yes and no?''

''It is better and not better.''

''There's a character for you, this Beria,'' Stalin said. ''He always leaves room for retreat. Mikhail Georgievich, I know that this is not very pleasant for you, but I would bend a little more, if I were you, when you play the role of the great Stalin. You are an observant person. I can already see the difference. You were such a little rooster when you came and now you're not. A considerable difference.''

"I am an actor, batono.''

"And as for this gesture. Mine is more modest and natural. You allow a certain pomposity to come through, something à la Napoleon. But I would like this gesture to go down in history as à la Stalin. Do you understand?'' Placing his right hand inside his tunic, Stalin added: "Please observe. Now, you do it. Yes, that's good, good. Very good. Excellent. It is both modest and at the same time masculine. Very good. You straighten and scratch your mustache properly.

"The final item: intonation. On this subject, I have no comments, your intonation is certainly Stalin's. You caught the pattern of my speech accurately. Is it permissible to ask, Mikhail Georgievich, have you unlearned how to speak like yourself, like Gelovani?''

"I am afraid I have unlearned to speak like myself, Josif Vissarionovich,'' Gelovani smiled with embarrassment.

Beria said with laughter:

"His poor wife! To have her own Stalin at home. That is not so easy, eh, batono?''

"All right, all right . . . How did you put it, Lavrenti Pavlovich? 'You cannot feed a nightingale a fairy tale?' That is a good saying. Yes, and in fact I invited you for dinner, Mikhail Georgievich, I asked you to wear the uniform of the generalissimo of the USSR, to be made-up like Stalin, and here I have criticized you. And read a scholarly work for three hours. Where is the food? Comrade Stalin, what kind of Georgian are you?''

Stalin pointed to the door with a broad gesture, and all three returned to the dining room. Thus began a long, traditional, sumptuous Georgian dinner, with an abundance of food, toasts, and songs.

"Fill the glasses with wine, Comrade Beria. That is your duty."

"With pleasure, Josif Vissarionovich, batono. I prefer that duty to all the rest, as you know."

"What a magnificent spread," Gelovani ventured.

"Georgian," Stalin said. "In your honor. I like the Russian people, but with respect to food on the table they know nothing. If you sat them down in front of such a table, they would not understand a thing. They would say there's too much grass. All they want is borsch and Piroshki. Try the dzhondzholi,* Mikhail Georgievich. Please help yourself."

Gelovani took an appetizer and the greens, unfolded the starched napkin and tucked one side behind the edge of his tunic. Stalin noticed this and grinned.

"Now that is something I do not do, batono, Misha. With the napkin. I usually put it on my lap. And, of course, sooner or later, I drop it on the floor."

"Forgive me, I did not know that." Gelovani placed the napkin on his lap.

"If it happens in Beria's presence, he, of course, picks it up," said Stalin.

"But if Mikhail Gelovani drops the napkin, Josif Vissarionovich, I will not pick it up," Beria joked.

"By the way, Mikhail Georgievich, is it true that you are from the aristocracy?" Stalin asked.

"Hm, you see, Josif Vissarionovich . . ." Gelovani an-

---

* A sour plant of Georgia, something like grass.

swered, "my father was an aristocrat, that's true. I studied in a classical secondary school . . ."

"I can see by your manners . . ."

"Mash, amkhanagebo!"* Beria exclaimed in a loud voice.

"Look at our marshal, Mikhail Georgievich. He is like a frisky horse before the final battle. He exercises his hooves with impatience."

"You cannot feed a nightingale a fairy tale. You said that yourself, Josif Vissarionovich!"

"You're right, you're right, Lavrenti. You know, Misha, despite everything, I love this Beria. And he trades on that, dammit! All right, comrades. The suggestion is to select Marshal Beria as our toastmaster. No objections? He has this at his fingertips. He knows all the Georgian customs and habits by heart. Accepted unanimously. Beria, you may direct your attention to the fulfillment of your duties."

"Thank you Comrade Stalin, for your trust. I will try to live up to it, this time as well. It seems to me that in the course of many, many years, the Leninist and Stalinist Beria has not deceived you."

"The second heir to the throne," Stalin said, with a smile.

"If I am the second, who is the first?"

Stalin continued to laugh and turned to Gelovani:

"You see what kind of questions he asks me. No, this courtier does not understand that he cannot have a claim to our Soviet throne. Listen, Marshal Beria, the Russian people cannot tolerate a second Georgian. Thank God, they still tolerate the first, me. Isn't that clear to you?"

---

* The Georgian expression for: "And so, comrades!"

"We were . . . we were just joking, weren't we?" Beria asked.

"In every joke there is an element of truth, you know. And I know very well what you dream of. . . ."

Early the next morning, when Rodionovna entered the dining room, she could not believe her eyes. The table was in total disorder; probably ten bottles of wine had been consumed. Beria, without jacket or shoes, was dancing the Caucasian lezginka, and Gelovani was tapping the chair rhythmically like a drum.

Stalin stood in the middle of the room with a horn in his hand, swaying as he proposed a toast.

"Comrades! I would like to drink out of this horn, which dates back to the time of Czar Iraklii . . . to drink not to the past, not to the czars and princes, but to our present-day *screw,* who serves us in the city and in the village. To the Soviet *screw,* comrades! The screws in our life solve everything. We, party and nonparty leaders, are worth nothing without screws. But often we forget about screws. And that is unforgivable. It is very bad! Is it permissible to ask, comrades, what is a screw? I answer for history: The Soviet screw is our brother, our sister, it is the common man in the city and in the village, carrying out his shared social work.

"Screws are not nails! I want our houses to be held together not by nails but by screws, because first of all, nails rust. And secondly, because they are too primitive for our times. . . . But screws, comrades, screws are a tricky thing. They are, you know, based on the principle of the spiral. Yes, yes, the spiral. The further you turn a screw, the stronger it becomes, comrades. I drink to our dear, our nice, our honest, our deeply patriotic, and deeply-devoted-to-

Comrade-Stalin, our Soviet—not nails, but screws!''

The leader slowly drank the wine from the horn. He drank ceremoniously, as was his custom. After that he turned the horn over; not a drop of wine remained.

Rodionovna could not help crossing herself.

"Oh, my God," she said.

Stalin staggered. And staggered again. But even though he was swaying slightly, he did not lose his balance. Beria and Gelovani, who were blind drunk, paid no attention to him. Rodionovna looked at the leader and waited. Was he going to fall or not?

The Doctor's Assistant

Akaki Tsirodze was eighty-four years old. His face looked like a baked apple. His ears were withered like autumn leaves, but his mustache stood out and was still reddish. He walked without a slouch. His voice had always been shrill like a woman's, so that was not from old age. When he played nardy* with his neighbor Mito Parkadze, a seventy-five-year-old giant and former spike driver at the railroad depot, he would say:

"My mother was born in Gudauta, and in Abkhazia people live to be 140. So there is still a long time before death.

It was after he had retired and moved to Grma-Geli on the outskirts of Tbilisi, where he and Mito had adjoining rooms sharing a terrace, that Akaki had a most unusual experience. Such things, it might be thought, could happen only in fairy tales.

Tsirodze, without warning, became the personal physi-

* An Oriental game popular in Georgia.

cian of the great Stalin. It is hard to believe, but Mito was a witness.

The fact was that the leader hated doctors. However, as secretary general of the Central Committee of the Soviet Communist party and leader of the international proletariat, he was forced to do what he did not like, to be examined by these "accursed Aesculapiuses and charlatans." He did not generally believe in the medical sciences; more important, he feared for his life, having grown paranoid as all great people do. This became particularly apparent when Marshal Beria "uncovered" several plots against party leaders and against Stalin himself. One of these plots turned out to have been instigated by the doctors of the Kremlin Medical Center who were planning to kill the Soviet rulers, or, to be more accurate, to poison them with medicines. So far, no one has proved, and now no one will ever be able to discover, whether these plots were real or of Beria's fabrication. The marshal, perhaps with the help of these plots, hoped to strengthen his shaky position, for Stalin had ceased to trust him and for a whole year had not allowed Beria access to himself.

In a word, the leader had rebelled and had told General Vlasek that he would no longer allow doctors to treat him. Nevertheless, he was not feeling well. Irregularity in heartbeat had become more frequent, sleep was gone forever, his bones ached, he even had trouble breathing, and his headaches, of course, gave him no peace.

One summer, after he had arrived at his *dacha* in Esheri, the leader decided to spend a week in the hunting cabin on Lake Ritsa. A cabin situated on an island had been built for him with all the amenities. As soon as Stalin came to rest on the shores of the Black Sea, life took on a Moscow cast. All roads were controlled by the state security officers, and there were majors and colonels on motorcycles and in cars, mostly in militia uniforms. Merchandise from the capital began to appear in stores. Newspapers of nearly six pages came out, and so on. It should be mentioned that Malenkov and Beria vacationed on the Black Sea at the same time, Malenkov in Sochi and Beria in Gagry.

When Stalin was at the cabin on Lake Ritsa and suffering from insomnia and headaches, he remembered Akaki Tsirodze, his former friend from Tiflis. The last time they had seen each other had been almost half a century earlier. That was when the young Dzhugashvili had just embarked on the path of a professional revolutionary. He worked at the Observatory. In the evenings he organized Marxist circles in Grma-Geli with the aim of inciting workers to overthrow the autocracy. It was in one of these circles that Stalin met the good-natured Tsirodze, a male nurse at the Railroad Hospital. Stalin had once caught a cold and had almost contracted pneumonia. Tsirodze cured him of his ailment in a jiffy. Stalin recalled Akaki's story of how he, a male nurse and only an assistant on the night shift, had amputated the leg of a locomotive driver after a railroad accident. This story, and of course, Stalin's desire to avoid professional doctors from the Kremlin Medical Center, brought him to the decision to seek out Akaki and make him his personal physician.

General Vlasek immediately called Rapava, the minister of state security of Georgia in Tbilisi. And in the course of twenty-four hours, with the help of his colleagues, he located Tsirodze. The latter was ordered both to have his hair cut and to shave. He came dressed in a dark suit. His dossier had, of course, been checked out and it was discovered that

Akaki had joined the Communist party at the beginning of the century, that he had served as male nurse at the Railroad Hospital all his life, and that he had never left the boundaries of Tiflis. Moreover, Rapava was amazed to find that Tsirodze had spent all those years in the same house in Grma-Geli.

Akaki was flown from Tbilisi to Sukhumi, and then was taken by car to Stalin on Lake Ritsa. There, in the wooden hunting cabin, the meeting between Tsirodze and the leader took place. They embraced, kissed, had dinner, drank, of course, and reminisced about the past. Later Stalin told Akaki:

"And now I want you to be with me. You are an old man and I am an old man. But you can treat me. Then treat me. I do not trust Moscow doctors. You were a good male nurse. You remember a few things you were taught."

But Akaki, if truth be known, remembered nothing of what he had been taught. His already limited medical knowledge had somehow flown from his head. Well, of course he remembered something, and it seemed to him that he remembered the main things, that in case of a stomach-ache an enema should be administered, that mustard plaster is a very good cure for headaches, and that for a cold, goat's fat should be rubbed onto the chest. He of course remembered how to apply cupping glasses, measure temperature, how to draw blood, and take blood pressure. And Akaki undoubtedly remembered that a normal pulse should not exceed 72 beats a minute. Yes, and Akaki also knew that for a sore throat it was good to drink hot Borzhomi with milk.

Stalin did not ask Tsirodze whether he wanted to be personal physician to the Great Leader, to say nothing of whether he was *capable* of being the personal physician to the Great Leader. He simply appointed him to fill the vacant spot. And for Stalin this was a great relief. He now had an old friend with him, an old man, and an old male nurse. That was safer than to have the luminaries from the capital at his side.

On the first night Stalin himself made up the bed in the guest room, and, after he tucked Akaki in, sat at the edge of the bed, just as he had sometimes done with his daughter, Svetlana, before she went to sleep. Stalin and Akaki even shed a few tears together.

Thus Tsirodze began to live with Stalin as a guardian to the king, or a brother to the minister, carrying out his duties as private physician. He was given an apartment in Moscow, a *dacha,* a secretary. He wore a white robe, and had offices in the Kremlin and at every Stalin *dacha.* A stethoscope appeared around his neck, and in his glass cabinet there was an endless supply of mustard plaster. When he was told he could order from abroad anything he wanted in the way of medical preparations, he answered proudly:

"No, I need nothing from them. I am a Soviet patriot and do not need capitalist things."

The leader thanked Akaki for these words.

But the most amazing thing is that from the moment Tsirodze became Stalin's personal physician, the latter began to feel noticeably better. He willingly drank hot Borzhomi with milk, accepted enemas, allowed his chest to be rubbed down with goat's fat, and took baths with mustard plaster.

Moreover, Akaki Tsirodze, whom some secretly called "the quack from Georgia," gained fame. With Stalin's permission, other officials of the party and government began going to him and he gave them enemas and rubbed down their chests with goat's fat.

Akaki seemed younger for all of this. He did, of course,

suffer because he could not play nardy with Mito, but this problem soon solved itself when he met one of Beria's guards, a Georgian who was also an avid player of nardy. They spent their Sundays together.

Still, there were several snags. Once, when the conversation centered on kidneys, Stalin had to explain to Akaki why in fact a person needs kidneys. And Akaki began to argue with the leader, trying to prove that a person can live without kidneys. He had obviously confused kidneys and appendixes.

It is interesting that when he was in Moscow, Akaki had access to the Kremlin hospital. With the help of the Kremlin doctors, he treated his hemorrhoids and lowered his blood pressure. Most important, his rotten teeth were extracted and excellent artificial teeth made from foreign materials were put in their place.

And so it turned out as follows: Professional doctors treated Akaki, and Akaki, a former male nurse, secretly called by some "the quack from Georgia," treated the Great Leader.

However, nothing under the sun lasts forever, as they say. Tsirodze's career ended as quickly as it had begun. Stalin suddenly began to suspect this old friend of evil thoughts. He stopped drinking Borzhomi with milk, prohibited goat's-fat rubdowns, and categorically refused mustard plasters. And all this because agents of the state security accidentally found Akaki's second cousin in Paris, someone named Isidore Tsirodze. He worked in a dairy store but had at one time issued an anti-Soviet leaflet in Georgian, which had been infiltrated into Georgia via Turkey. Even though Akaki had never heard of this second cousin, Stalin one fine day angrily called Akaki an "Aesculapion'' and a charlatan and ordered General Vlasek to pack him up and send him to his place of permanent residence in Grma-Geli. (Thank God he was not sent somewhere like Siberia.)

Yes, Akaki was sent back to Georgia. And Stalin again began to have headaches, he again suffered from insomnia, and again had irregularity in heartbeat.

Akaki is still alive and healthy. He is now ninety-four-years old, he continues to play nardy with Mito, and he continues to say:

"My mother was born in Gudauta, and in Abkhazia people live to be 140. So there is still a long time before death."

God only knows, perhaps he will last to 140, for the Kremlin doctors had rid him of his hemorrhoids, his high blood pressure, and had put in new teeth. All this, but first, of course, there was his mother's Abkhazian milk.

At His Wife's Grave

This time the meeting of the government commission was held in Stalin's business office and began at noon. The chairman of the State Planning Committee, two ministers, and four venerable scientists were seated at a long table.

The academician Sevrikov, a middle-aged man with a thin, pedantic face, who always supported Stalin's proposals, came forward. He waved his left arm slightly, in an automatic and dispassionate gesture, and said something about ground structure in the district in which a canal was being planned. His words were clipped, and sounded like the keys of a typewriter. This irritated Stalin, who was pacing from one end of the office to the other. He was smoking, in fact blowing smoke rings. He made no attempt to grasp the meaning of what Sevrikov was saying, knowing that the latter was an obedient, well-disciplined, and useful person. Inwardly, Stalin was bothered by the academician Zamorsky, an old man with a pointed beard like Trotsky's, gray, bushy eyebrows, and a cynical look about the eyes. It seemed to him that Zamorsky always regarded him with a slight sneer, as though to say: "Eh, leader, leader, all your projects are rubbish—they're not worth a cent."

Zamorsky did not, of course, say this aloud, but Stalin could not help feeling uncomfortable, even though he knew very well that no one would dare come out against his projects. In the last years of his life they had become an obsession. One great Stalin building project after another. Canals were dug, man-made seas were formed, underground military cities were built, and new railroads were laid, to mention only some of the projects.

Enormous sums of money were spent. All this became history in Stalin's lifetime. Front-page stories were written about these novelties, these "Stalin reformations." Although mostly senseless, they created a furor. The Soviet press called it the great socialist constructive labor, which united the people and kept them on their guard as if it were the peaceful continuation of revolution. That was what Stalin hoped to achieve and he was proud of it, but occasionally when he caught Zamorsky's cynical expression (and there were other Zamorskys), he began to feel uncertain, as though all his projects were really rubbish, as though they were self-indulgences, perhaps even caprices.

Whenever this thought came into Stalin's mind, he shuddered, because it made him feel like an ordinary sinful mortal. And if you think about it, who in this case could have separated out sensible reform from rubbish and caprice? Suddenly the feeling of omnipotence and mission, the assurance of intellectual superiority, all that by which Stalin defined himself as genius (and he basically believed in genius), abandoned him and fear took over. Was he not committing an irreversible crime? Was he not building a house of cards? Was he molding a colossus with feet of clay? To put it simply: Was he a charlatan? These insidious questions crept into his head.

What if Zamorsky, deep down, considered him to be a charlatan? What if Zamorsky and others, even though they carried out what was demanded of them, regarded all of these "Stalin reformations" as bluffs? The leader understood that the main question at issue was whether his deeds immortalized him as a genius or as a schemer and tyrant.

He had read somewhere that Czar Alexander I (Stalin did not distinguish between the Russian czars very well, even though he had overthrown the last one almost single-handedly), having thought up the idea of constructing a railroad between St. Petersburg and Moscow, summoned his ministers and, pointing to the map, said: "I want this railroad to be straight as an arrow. Like this." And the czar placed the pencil on the map so that one end touched St. Petersburg and the other end Moscow. This pencil of the czar's cost the Russian people tens of thousands of lives, because the railroad line had to be laid in unsuitable places. Marshlands and swamps had to be filled in, hills had to be leveled, and forests had to be chopped down.

Well, no one could say that Stalin was fool enough to insist that this new 1,000-kilometer canal to Central Asia be dug in a straight line.

He felt a slight weakness in his legs and a sharp, fleeting pain in his left shoulder blade, and he lowered himself into a chair. For a moment his vision was blurry. Sevrikov noticed this and faltered in his presentation. The chairman of the Gosplan looked worriedly at Stalin.

"It's nothing, nothing, continue, Comrade Sevrikov," Stalin said.

He had felt weakness in his legs before, and the quick but sharp pain in his shoulder blade as well. He had also experienced the unsettling possibility that everything he was doing might not be sound, and this lingering doubt had shaken his belief in the infallibility of himself as the wise government leader and helmsman of a new course.

One more thing: At times it seemed to Stalin that all his "great socialist constructions" were due to the fact that in recent years he had begun to fear death. Previously he had not feared death. Death had not been standing on the threshold. But now it was different. The leader tried with all his might to avoid thinking of death, but the thought would worm its way into his brain and take over. It came against his will and could be controlled only with great effort. The closer Stalin came to the end of his earthly existence (and he did not believe in a paradise after death, although he sometimes tried very hard), the more often and more persistently he was obsessed by the frightening concept of nonbeing, a concept not subject to analysis.

This was spiritually unsettling to him, a feeling unlike anything else. He could not answer the simple question: How is it that everything on earth will remain, will live, except me? And the only salvation from this emotional turmoil was accelerated daily activity, involvement in the process of creating, work, work, useful work, or useless work—but work. Even a condemned man will, while digging a grave for himself, get carried away momentarily by the work itself and forget the end result.

Didn't Egyptian Pharaohs erect those gigantic pyramids out of fear of death? Wasn't this construction an act of faith in immortality? Stalin had read of this and he wanted to believe that immortality existed not only in children, as Leo Tolstoi contended, but also in fame, in immortalizing yourself through the history of mankind.

All these psychological threads would become entangled and drive Stalin to despair, as again and again he was forced to admit to a power stronger than himself, a force independent of his will. And this Stalin hated, because it was in direct contradiction to Marxist philosophy, which had not reconciled itself to death.

He would tell himself that work is stronger than death. That was an attractive idea. At one time he had liked to say that love is stronger than death. And that had sounded attractive, too. But, alas, words could not transcend the fact of physical mortality. Words remained words.

More and more frequently, during the last years of his life, Stalin came to the conclusion that all things were meaningless and mortal. And this made him furious because it was the same pessimistic view expressed by bourgeois philosophers against those who demanded social changes and equality. "Why do all of this when death is inevitable?" they asked.

The meeting was interrupted as Poskrebyshev came into the office, slouched over, moving clumsily. He approached Stalin and his voice brought the leader back to reality.

"Josif Vissarionovich, Svetlana is on the telephone," he said softly. "Will you talk to her?"

Stalin wanted to get angry at his daughter for calling at the wrong time, but hearing the name Svetlana cheered him up. It was like the straw to which a drowning man clings. The existence of his daughter awakened his instinct toward life and lessened his fear of death. Stalin got up from his chair, went over to his desk, and picked up the city phone.

"Hello, my skylark. How are you? Ah?" he said cheerfully and affectionately.

For five minutes, the leader spoke with his daughter.

Svetlana wanted to visit her father at his *dacha* on the following Sunday, with her husband and children. Stalin agreed to this immediately. Then he asked her about her job at the Institute of World Literature and discussed other trivialities.

Those present at the meeting examined their papers in silence, as though to emphasize that they were not interested in the telephone conversation. Sevrikov even sat down.

"Are there any instructions, Josif Vissarionovich?" Poskrebyshev asked after Stalin had hung up.

"No, none. You may go, Comrade Poskrebyshev."

Poskrebyshev left. Stalin returned to his chair, smiled warmly and noted:

"Someone once said: 'Children are the flowers of life.' Continue, Comrade Sevrikov."

Sevrikov returned to ground structures, but the leader was not listening. He was thinking of his daughter because it was pleasant to think of her. Stalin could not be proud of his son, who was a drunkard, but Svetlana was a fine girl. Even though she had little luck with husbands. On Sundays, she generally visited her father at his *dacha,* with her second husband, Yuri Zhdanov, the son of Andrei Zhdanov, whom Stalin respected and valued as much as he was capable of respecting or valuing anyone. The divorce with Grigori Morozov (Moroz) had to some extent been encouraged by the leader, and it's possible that he insisted on Svetlana's marriage to Yuri. By all evidence, she did not appear to be happy with the young and talented scholar and party man. Stalin had advanced him to a leading position in the Central Committee, but this changed nothing. Svetlana was probably right: Yuri was a bureaucrat and careerist, even though he was gifted, having inherited a great deal from his father. Stalin felt a vague sense of blame when he thought of his daughter's future and of his grandchildren, and in general he was in agreement with Svetlana. As a rule, children of party leaders grew up to be riffraff.

No, the leader did not see any real love between his daughter and Zhdanov's son. No, there did not exist between them what had been between Stalin and his second wife, Nadezhda Alliluyeva.

As he thought of his wife, the leader became anxious and tense. Svetlana resembled her mother. When she spoke she was a carbon copy of Nadezhda. Stalin closed his eyes for a moment and before him appeared the image of his favorite woman, who had so senselessly and tragically departed from life.

Abruptly Stalin rose and interrupted Sevrikov:

"Comrades, we are beating the air, as the Russian saying goes. Let's wind up the discussion of the project. The main points are clear. Tomorrow, the Council of Ministers will pass a resolution to build the new canal. You can talk over the details by yourselves, in an orderly fashion."

The meeting was adjourned. No one protested. But Zamorsky again looked sneeringly at Stalin, as though he understood that it was not the canal that interested Stalin now, but something else.

When Stalin was alone in his office, he opened the safe and took out a photograph of a pretty young woman, which he always kept near him. For some time he had kept it in the safe. The photograph had been taken in the twenties and had yellowed slightly. Nadezhda was looking straight into the camera. There was a happy smile on her face. Her eyes were sparkling, so familiar, so dear to Stalin. And the chestnut hair, which he liked so much to run his hand through. Nadezhda had a coat with a fur collar, and she was wearing a beret on her head. The beret had been sent to her by someone from Berlin.

He held the picture of his wife and gazed at it as millions of widowers have, simple ordinary men who loved their wives. Nadezhda and he had met for the first time in foggy St. Petersburg, at the apartment of the veteran Russian revolutionary, the proletarian Alliluyev. Stalin was already Lenin's collaborator and was involved in the full danger of underground work. This was before the October Revolution. Nadezhda, who had been brought up to believe as her father did, also took part in conspiratorial affairs, and was courageous and resourceful. Indeed, it was a conspiracy that brought them together. There was something romantic about it. Nadezhda fell in love with Stalin at first sight, the way it happens in romantic novels. Stalin was, however, convinced that a true revolutionary must be an ascetic. Fortunately, love overcame this conviction. Stalin's sense of realism, of course, assisted in this change of attitude; his capacity for realism never left him.

Stalin had loved his first wife, Keke Svanidzhe, as only a Georgian can love, passionately and a bit ostentatiously. He did not know her well, and they had lived together for just a short time. She died suddenly, leaving a son, Stalin's first child, Yasha. It could be said that women did not play an essential role in Stalin's life before he met Nadezhda. There were, of course, isolated episodes, but they were not binding and they led to nothing.

Nadezhda Alliluyeva was a true wife to Stalin, a friend, the person whom he needed most of all of those who surrounded him. And they loved each other.

Stalin called Poskrebyshev and said to him:

"Listen, tell them to have everything in readiness. In half an hour I am going to Novo-Deviche Cemetery."

Poskrebyshev nodded, for he understood that the leader had decided to visit his wife's grave.

The Novo-Deviche Cemetery, which is so well known to Muscovites, deserves a few words. This is the place where under tombstones the best representatives of the Russian intelligentsia of the previous era lie, including Anton Chekhov. During the Soviet period this cemetery became the burial ground for the most privileged members of the elite society: government and party bigwigs, marshals and generals, all kinds of popular artists, famous writers, film directors, and so on. Properly speaking, after Novo-Deviche, the next step up is the Kremlin wall. The archbigwig can either be entombed in the wall or buried beside it. The ultimate step is Lenin's Mausoleum, but only one Lenin lies in it; even Stalin was able to lie next to him for only a short time.

So one can understand that to obtain two meters of land in the Novo-Deviche Cemetery is not such a simple matter. They say that these cemetery plots sit there as though they were lying fallow, in other words, they are under the Kremlin control. A special government commission is said to preside over each individual case to decide which honorable body should be allotted a grave. Rumor has it that sometimes the graves are *not* allotted and that the worthiness of such and such honorable corpse is thereby diminished. It is also said that voting takes place in this special commission secretly. If a certain corpse does not receive the necessary vote, then, first of all, shame has been cast on that person's former services, and secondly, he will be buried in some Godforsaken place outside Moscow, such as Lyubertsy.

As soon as General Vlasek heard that Stalin was planning to go to Novo-Deviche, he called his men at the cemetery—there were permanent guards stationed there—and ordered that the cemetery be cleared of all other people. When Stalin's car and the escort entered the gates of the cemetery from Pirogorsky Street, it was empty. Vlasek accompanied the leader to Alliluyeva's grave, which was located directly to the right of the gates. Stalin was wearing a gray gabardine coat with the shoulder strap of the generalissimo, buttoned all the way up to the top, and a military cap. He sat down on a marble bench and indicated by his expression that he wanted to be left alone. Vlasek moved away.

The wind gently stirred among the cypress trees. It was autumn.

Stalin gazed at the austere monument, with its bust of Nadezhda at the top. He liked its simplicity and expression. The dark marble emphasized the dignity and purity that were so characteristic of his wife and that drove her to her grave. The inscription on the tombstone read: "To Nadezhda Alliluyeva from a member of the Communist party, J. Stalin." For some reason this inscription had always bothered Stalin, even though he had ordered it to be carved on the stone. At times, that part of himself that he considered mystical raised the question: Why say "from a member of the Communist party" and not, "from J. Stalin," or simply "from your loving husband," as was done for centuries? But Stalin and Nadezhda had not been simply husband and wife; they had been friends, comrades, and, of course, like-minded people. Or were they like-minded?

At that moment Stalin heard voices shouting, someone's rapid breathing, the sounds of a chase. Then a girl about six or seven years old ran within the boundaries of Alli-

luyeva's grave. She had a turned-up nose and freckles. Her
eyes were full of fear and she was crying. Her clothes were
plain. On her feet were worn-out sandals and socks with
holes. Almost falling, she threw herself at Stalin, seized
him around the knees. Two majors from Stalin's guards
came puffing up, the big and husky Shchetkin, and the
short-legged, jowly Chichko. Shchetkin had a revolver in
his hand. Both men were in a state, obviously determined to
take the most extreme measures. When they reached for the
girl, Stalin said sternly:

"Don't touch her."

Vlasek then appeared on the scene.

"What happened here?" Stalin demanded. Not waiting
for an answer, he said gently to the girl: "Don't cry, button-
nose, don't cry. These men won't harm you. They are good
men. Don't be afraid. Now tell me, button-nose, what happened? How did you end up here?"

As he bent down to wipe the girl's nose with his own
handkerchief, Stalin recalled how Svetlana as a little girl
also had lots of freckles. Often had a runny nose, too.
The child's body shook. She clung to Stalin's knees and
convulsively squeezed his left hand with her fingers. The
tears in her eyes quickly dried, but the fear seemed to be
fixed.

It turned out that the guards had discovered the girl plant-
ing flowers at one of the neighboring graves. When she saw
the majors, she had become terrified and run in the direction
of Alliluyeva's grave. She had not understood that the bells
ringing throughout the cemetery meant that all visitors must
leave immediately. The girl's mother worked in the management office of the cemetery, and since she had no one to
leave her daughter with, she let the girl spend the day plant-

ing flowers at the graves. She was too young to go to school.

"What is your name?" Stalin asked.

"Masha . . . Rumyantseva," the girl answered. "And what is your name, uncle with the mustache?"

"Stalin."

The girl frowned and did not at first believe him.

"You are Uncle Stalin? Our Stalin?" she asked.

The leader nodded.

"Yes, Mashenka, I am your Stalin," he said. "Your Stalin."

Impetuously the girl embraced Stalin and kissed him on the cheek. Vlasek lowered his eyes, but Stalin returned the embrace and kissed the girl on the cheek as well. By this time, the two majors had left the boundaries of Alliluyeva's grave, for they understood that there was nothing for them to do.

"Well, then, Mashenka," said Stalin, "you will be taken to your mother now. Tomorrow I will send you some fruit and toys. Do you like dolls?"

"I like Teddy bears," Mashenka said cheerfully. "Mama said she would buy me one a long time ago, but there's never enough money."

"You will have a Teddy bear, Mashenka. Tomorrow you will have a Teddy bear," Stalin promised. "It will be from Uncle Stalin."

(The next day, Mashenka received a basket of fruit and a red-haired Teddy bear that was as tall as she was.)

The leader sat alone on the marble bench in front of the grave. He could not forget the look of fear in Mashenka's eyes. Had he ever seen such a frightened child before? What had caused her fear?

Suddenly the inscription on the tombstone—"To Nadezhda Alliluyeva from a member of the Communist party, J. Stalin"—seemed stupid and pompous to him. For one thing, when he had ordered the inscription, he had not been simply a member of the Communist party, but the secretary general of the Central Committee. The inscription should have read: "From the secretary general of the Central Committee." Why had he played such a modest and unassuming role? What nonsense!

Stalin looked angrily at this inscription. He wanted to erase it with the heel of his boot. He would have it changed from that idiotic and pretentious wording, "from a member of the Communist party," and simply have "from J. Stalin."

The fear that he had seen in Mashenka's eyes still tormented him. Again he thought of his wife. What had brought her to that catastrophic end?

"Nadya . . . why did you do it?" he said aloud.

The memory of that ill-fated night came back to him. Actually, there had been a combination of factors that had accumulated over time; according to the laws of Marxism, a quantitative difference at a certain moment can be transformed into a qualitative difference. But Stalin felt that if that night had been different, Nadezhda would not have shot herself the next day with the small pistol. He sighed. Yes, a deep spiritual and intellectual conflict had permeated all aspects of their relationship, even the most intimate. The closeness between them had come to an end and all his efforts to renew it came to naught. For the first time he had realized that a woman cannot be a woman if she has lost respect for the man she loves.

Stalin had often been cruel to his wife. This was in line

with his character. He made fun of her and he made fun of others, and Nadya would get angry. She would even stop talking to him, or call him a Georgian pig. But in the end, she would forgive him. That was when she still respected him as a person and as a Leninist.

Perhaps it all started when she entered the Institute of Red Professorship, or perhaps it was earlier. Probably it all began with arrests. Nadya supported Stalin in his fight against the opposition, during the time of debate. She supported him even when several "on the left" and "on the right" were expelled from the party. But she was against terror. Then the mass arrests took place. People who could not be suspected of treason were taken away, even though the first victory over the opposition had been won and Trotsky had been sent beyond the Soviet borders. And Nadezhda's close relatives had been arrested.

She could not reconcile herself to this. She reproached Stalin, as secretary general of the party, for unwarranted cruelty. On the night in question she called him a murderer. She could not understand that it was impossible to have progress without widespread terror, that it was necessary to crush the strength, not only of the opposition, but also of the remaining class enemies who had adapted themselves to the new conditions. Nadezhda was an idealist. She believed in debate, in exchange of ideas, in convictions. She talked endlessly about the strength of Lenin's bequests to us. At the same time, she asked if Stalin really liked to arrest those who were close to him. Did he not feel pity for them deep in his heart, and did he not feel sorry for himself and curse his own zeal? No, Nadezhda did not understand. Or she didn't want to understand.

Having convinced himself that he was right and she was

wrong, Stalin felt that he would become like that Russian czar who had built the railroad between St. Petersburg and Moscow. He feared this parallel, even though it was apt. In truth, he preferred a comparison between himself and Christ. Hadn't Christ tried to lead his people toward improvement, toward perfection, toward good and happiness? And look how much blood had been spilled over Christ!

The dialectic teaches that in each action the counteraction is hidden, and the one gives rise to the other. Good accompanies evil, in the same way that evil accompanies good. Does not the history of mankind confirm this fact, and do not all the great progressive beginnings have to be paid for by blood? In order to accomplish something good, something evil must also be done. Stalin believed in this natural law, because it was convenient for him to do so, because it freed his hands, because it removed the possibility of reproach for his "Asian character," "stubbornness," and "caprice," and because it conformed to the age-old saying: "If the forest is cut, chips will fly." Of course Stalin never thought about what would happen to him if he should turn out to be one of the repressed.

Now he realized that the fear he had seen in the child's eyes was like what he had seen in the eyes of his beloved wife. On that dreadful night, when she had confessed to him all that was on her mind, when she called him a murderer, when he couldn't control himself and had slapped her in the face, when she had sobbed and fallen face down on the bed. If only he had asked for her forgiveness on that awful night instead of leaving her and going to Moscow. If only he could have had one more chance to convince her that there was nothing he could do, that he was prisoner of Lenin's ideas, which controlled him. He did not want to kill people, but had to. If he had been able to explain all that, perhaps Nadya would not have shot herself.

Tears stung the leader's eyes. He wiped them away with his finger and frowned. Dammit, what sentimentality! Since when did Stalin shed tears? That had never happened before. It was old age. And that damned mysticism.

Then a thought began to form in his mind. If, after Nadezhda's suicide, his heart had hardened even more, and if he had ordered more people killed after her suicide than before, it was *because* of Nadya. She was to blame, it was she who had embittered him, and he had probably acted in retaliation. Perhaps that phrase about Ivan IV and the Time of Troubles first appeared on his lips at this time.

In the car with Vlasek on the way back to the Kremlin, Stalin's thoughts returned to Zamorsky, that nasty little old man whose eyes always seemed to be saying, "Eh, leader, leader, all your projects are rubbish—they're not worth a cent." As he thought of Zamorsky he again felt a slight weakness in his legs, and that horrible sharp but momentary pain shot through his left shoulder. He cried out to himself: "So this is how the end comes, suddenly and unexpectedly. It could happen anywhere, even in this car." It was no less painful to realize that perhaps Zamorsky was right. We are mortal, life is meaningless, and people will forget Stalin just as easily as they have forgotten Alexander Makedonsky, and Napoleon, and many others. After all, what is time? Isn't one thousand years just a day in a span that covers billions of years?

A feeling of emptiness and loss came over him. The feeling persisted and became almost physical, giving him pain like an ulcer or a wound does. Suddenly he addressed Vlasek, who was sitting next to the chauffeur: "Hey, you, I want the inscription on my wife's grave changed, the inscription on the tombstone, that is. Do you know what I'm talking about? It says 'from a member of the Communist party.' That must be removed. Let it say 'from J. Stalin.' ''

"It will be done," Vlasek answered.

The next day, when Stalin was in the Kremlin, he summoned Poskrebyshev and said to him:

"Listen, Poskrebyshev, yesterday I ordered Vlasek to change the inscription on Nadezhda Alliluyeva's tombstone. Well, I have reconsidered. Let it stay the way it is. Tell Vlasek about this. I haven't seen him today. I think it's his day off."

Well, Mashenka Rumyantseva grew up, finished school, and entered the College of Mines. When she turned twenty, a group of friends, students and a few instructors, gathered at her hostel. And it happened that Stalin was mentioned in the course of the conversation. One of the instructors voiced a most disrespectful opinion of him, and another said that Stalin was a dictator, a petty tyrant who had done the Soviet Union a great deal of harm. The rest of the students remained silent. Many years had gone by. What did they know about Stalin?

Mashenka was silent too. She remembered how her mother had told her that her father had been arrested in 1948 and exiled to Magadan in the Far East, from which he had never returned. Her mother had said plainly:

"It was Stalin who killed your father, Masha. And for nothing."

She recalled this conversation, but she had lost her father when she was four years old, and she hardly remembered him. However, she remembered the red-haired Teddy bear all her life. It still sat on her bed. The other girls had laughed at her and accused her of "bourgeoisism," but she loved her Teddy bear and never told anyone where it came from.

Death

Don't kid yourself, I waited for it every day. And I was not the only one. Everyone waited. For death, that is, raw-boned death. The old man was seven and a half decades old. Somewhere I read that the average person lives to age seventy-four. It was time. He creaked all over. I myself noticed that his eyes were sometimes covered with a haze, and he walked on our mother earth unsteadily, like a child.

Every day I waited for raw-boned death.

I waited and shivered. I shivered for myself. It was a matter of life and death. Wouldn't you get shivers, if you were the head of Stalin's security, the chief of the first directorate of the Ministry of State Security, a general, and a member of the Communist party since 1921? How could I know which way things would go after the old man died?

So I sat in my office at the ministry, in March it was. I was sitting, working, when suddenly Colonel Kashkin called on the ''Kremlin line'' from the Blizhnaya *dacha*. He was my deputy, in charge of guarding the leader. He was usually on duty at Stalin's *dachas*.

He called and said:

"One way or the other, Comrade General, allow me to report. We are all in a state of alarm. He went to sleep at 3:35 A.M., and it is now after one in the afternoon, but there is silence in his study and the door, as usual, is locked from the inside. This has never happened before. He has never slept until two in the afternoon."

"Are you sure that he went to sleep in his study?" I asked.

"To be sure, Comrade General," Kashkin answered, "we are convinced of it. We have checked all the other rooms. He is there, in the study. There is no doubt."

"Let's wait one more hour," I suggested. "Call me in an hour. All right?"

After I hung up the receiver I felt weak and my stomach started playing tricks on me. The palms of my hands were perspiring. That was rare for me. I am a disciplined person. Stern. Nothing can surprise me. I remembered how the old man had nodded his head and said to me recently:

"Eh, Vlasek, they will hang you, my followers and comrades, by your feet after I die. And for nothing. You are a good soldier. You are a soldier and you will die like a soldier. This is why I promoted you."

I couldn't help asking:

"Why should they hang me, Josif Vissarionovich?"

"My kittens hate me, Vlasek," he said. "So you'd be better off running to America now and publishing your memoirs there. The imperialists will shower you with gold."

After an hour, Kashkin called again.

"What shall we do, Comrade General? There are no signs of life in his study."

I became angry.

"Why are you in such a panic over there, colonel?"

But in a half hour I was at Blizhnaya myself and was personally convinced that Kashkin had reason for alarm. The leader's study was locked from the inside. I knocked lightly on the door. There was no answer. I knocked a bit harder. Again no answer. Then I called the study from the living room on the rotator. No answer. Again, I felt weak. My stomach was queasy, and the palms of my hands were perspiring. However, in the presence of Kashkin and the guards I tried not to give myself away. I even whispered something like:

"Maybe the leader drank vodka yesterday, and is so far gone that a cannon wouldn't wake him up."

No one smiled.

I decided to call Malenkov at the Central Committee. He heard me out, and after a short pause (probably his stomach was queasy, too), he said:

"I'll be right there."

Next I called Beria. He was now deputy chairman of the Council of Ministers, so I called him at the Kremlin. His assistant informed me that Beria had left ten minutes earlier for Blizhnaya. So he sensed something, I thought, the son of a bitch. Who told him, the devil only knows. That one has his men everywhere! (Later I heard that Beria had made a comment somewhat like mine: "The old man probably drank too much wine and is rolling around on the floor." It is true that the leader had started to drink several months before his death, even though he knew it was bad for him.)

So they all gathered. Our whales gathered. The members of the Presidium of the Central Committee, the ten most deserving. The other members did not even show up. For

some reason the old man had recently expanded the Politburo and had then given it a new name—Presidium. Malenkov, with his elephant legs and puffy face, presided.

"Comrades," he said. "There is only one question before us: How shall we open the door to Comrade Stalin's
study? What are your suggestions and opinions?"

The big, baggy, Kaganovich, glancing timidly around,
said that a locksmith should be called to break down the
door.

Molotov, pushing his chin toward his smoked-through
mustache, said:

"But what if Comrade Stalin is sleeping? Personally, I
think he is sleeping."

"Yes, yes, of course, sleeping," Kaganovich said.

Almost everyone said in unison:

"He's sleeping, he's sleeping, he's sleeping."

Beria, waving his pawlike hands as though he were at a
Caucasian bazaar, demanded that any decision by the Presidium (they called this the narrow Presidium) should be
voted upon, and he said that he would recognize only a
unanimous vote. Beria was very active then, and I began to
suspect that perhaps he had sent our leader back to his great-
grandfathers. Beria was capable of anything. The old man
might have been poisoned. Beria had his own men everywhere, even though I was the chief of Stalin's security.

Nikita Khrushchev, who was round as a ball, with sly
peasant eyes like those of kulaks, made a suggestion that
received a unanimous vote.

"Who needs a locksmith," he said. "Let's push it in ourselves, all together."

They pushed it in, all together. The door popped open
like a cork. They flew into Stalin's study, all together. As
chief of security I was also allowed in.

What a merry-go-round! Just to think about it makes my heart sink.

Stalin lay on the floor in the uniform of the generalissimo of the USSR, and did not move. His face was white, his eyes rolled back. Something like foam bubbled on his lips. We froze. Who could have imagined a moment like this? No one. Here lay the leader, not moving. He could no longer do anything. Previously, he could do everything. That is why everyone feared him. And now? What would happen now?

Apparently no one had thought of approaching the corpse and lifting it to the couch. I took a step forward, but Khrushchev stepped in front of me. He knelt beside Stalin, put his ear to the leader's chest and announced:

"He is dead."

Kaganovich at once shouted:

"Who said Comrade Stalin is dead? I didn't."

"I didn't say it either," Molotov said.

They all began to yell:

"And I didn't say it!"

Malenkov shook his head.

"Comrades, the meeting of the Presidium proceeds," he said in a loud voice. "I suggest that first we strengthen security at the Kremlin and at all state institutions, and then call a doctor. Who is for that? Let's vote."

Everyone voted for. Then Malenkov said to me:

"The Presidium prohibits you from taking any photographs without the permission of the Presidium."

Strengthen the security around the Kremlin and all state institutions! Not a bad suggestion. But what was there to strengthen? We have an entire army for security. There was a ditch ten meters wide around each of Stalin's *dachas,* and deep in those ditches specially trained German shepherds walked. Who needs more than that?

All right. I was given the order to strengthen security. I accepted the order.

They sent for a doctor, in fact not one but a whole commission. As it turned out, the leader was not dead. (In his panic, Khrushchev was mistaken, or was it wishful thinking.) But he was in critical condition and unconscious.

During this dark moment, in front of the "corpse" of the great Stalin, I saw how the members of the narrow Presidium began, among themselves, to decide the future of the country. Malenkov and Beria, who unexpectedly formed an alliance, headed the discussion from one side. Molotov and everyone else represented the other side. At first, neither side wanted to include Khrushchev. He ran from Malenkov to Molotov, and from Molotov to Beria, and from Beria to Voroshilov, and whispered to everyone. Later, Malenkov and Beria took him in, and Molotov did not protest.

Meantime, the old man lay there, not yet willing to give up his last breath. And they bargained over who would get what post! I mean to say, who would *grab* what post.

In the end, to my misfortune, Beria obtained complete control of state security. When I heard this, I, an atheist, began to pray to God: "If only I may succeed in peacefully retiring, with a general's personal pension, and continue to use the apartment in Moscow and the *dacha* in Arkhangelskoe. That is all I want. I would occupy myself with photography and fishing."

What more did I need? I had had a difficult life, I had seen many things. I had started as a private and achieved the rank of general. With my past, I could write my memoirs. However, I am not literate enough to write memoirs, and besides, it's rather risky. So I thought I would catch fish, or hunt mushrooms in the forest.

Finally, God did not help me. He did not help the other officers in the leader's guard. Beria sent everyone off to Satan's grandmother, so to speak.

Lelya, You Don't Know Them

I was once a good comic actor. I played in theaters in Soviet Georgia; I played Molière, Beaumarchais, Goldoni, Shakespeare, and our own Georgian classics. I was liked. Yes, the audience enjoyed my performances. I was even famous. This was all before that memorable moment when Mikhail Chiaurelli, the film director, invited me to play the role of Stalin in *The Great Glow*. How could I refuse such an offer?

It is no easy matter, playing the role of the leader of the international proletariat, Vladimir Lenin's number-one pupil. Of course I accepted, and I played the role. To my own misfortune, I played the role successfully and was praised by the party critics, comrades from the Central Committee, and Stalin himself. From then on, my career as a comic actor was over. After that, I played only the role of Stalin, in the most diverse films, and, believe me, many were made.

You might say that the actor in me—in the best sense of the word—had died. In turn I received titles, honors, prizes. I became rich and was well known throughout the USSR.

But what will happen to me now that the Great Leader is dead? He died three days ago, leaving the country in deep mourning.

I don't know what will become of me.

I sat at home in my Moscow apartment on Gorki Street and read *Pravda,* all the pages of which had a black border and were devoted to the memory of the Great Leader. The radio was broadcasting the funeral marches of Chopin and Beethoven.

An odd sensation came over me. I had so grown into Stalin's role that I sometimes felt I had transformed myself into another person. I had stopped being the actor Mikhail Gelovani and had become the great Stalin. While this was dangerous during the leader's life, now it was somehow pathological. It seemed to me that I was dead, that I did not exist and everything in *Pravda* was about me. The funeral marches were "crying" over me, and the entire country was in mourning for me.

My wife, Lelya, came home. She is Ukrainian, a very capable woman, a singer by profession. She carried a large shopping bag filled with food. I helped her with her coat, and hung it up in the front hall. Lelya fixed her lovely hair and said:

"Darling, all those lines. Lines everywhere."

I couldn't understand why she went to the usual stores, for we could order everything that we needed by phone, from the special Kremlin food center and from a Georgian restaurant called Aragvi.

"People have lost their minds. They're all running. They act as though the world is coming to an end."

"That's almost the case, my dear," I said, falling into the tone of *Pravda*.

"You mean Stalin's death?"

I nodded and sighed.

"Our poor beloved Stalin," we both said.

Then my wife began to compare these days with the beginning of the war, when people were rushing around buying up matches, kerosene, sugar, and whatever they could, foreseeing shortages and famine. But why were they buying up matches, salt and soap now? Did they really anticipate disaster following Stalin's death?

"Oh, yes, Misha," Lelya suddenly remembered something. "On the Okhotny line I met Zagorodsky's wife. He did that gigantic statue of Stalin. She told me that terrible rumors are floating around Moscow."

"What rumors?" I naturally pricked up my ears. "Are Americans going to drop an atom bomb on us?"

"No, no, nothing like that."

"Is it permissible to ask, then, like what?"

"There you go again with your 'is it permissible.' You don't have to copy Stalin any more. He's dead. She told me that our 'luminaries' have been mobilized. She heard that from her husband, and he was told by a bigwig from the Central Committee. Everyone who knows about embalming has been summoned. Experts, specially picked by Mao Tse-tung, have been flown in from China. All of them did what they could, but Stalin's corpse won't respond to embalming."

"What?"

Something in me snapped. I felt a momentary spasm in my brain. I was probably the only person who could understand how frightening it was to hear Lelya's words. To tell you the truth, I could not think, instinct had completely suppressed reason.

"What's the matter, darling, is it your heart?" Lelya asked nervously.

Scarcely hearing my own voice, I shouted:

"Pack the suitcases! Right away! We'll take just what we need. Forget everything else."

I began running around the room like a madman. I grabbed something from the table, raced into the bedroom, pulled some underwear out of the dresser, and then headed for the desk, where I kept money, "in case." I had somehow foreseen that "in case." Lelya followed me, shrugging her shoulders and waving her hands.

"What's happened to you, Misha?" she kept asking me.

I yelled at her, called her a fool and an idiot. I had lost control. Without arguing, Lelya brought out two suitcases and began to pack my underwear.

"Where are we going? And why?" she asked.

"We are going to fly out of Moscow today."

"Where will we land?"

"Wherever our eyes take us. On the devil's horns, if necessary. Georgia. Crimea. Wherever you want. But we must go today, otherwise it will be too late!"

Lelya began to cry.

"Misha, Mishenka, tell me what has happened, I beg of you."

I sat her down.

"Don't you understand? Instead of Stalin, they will put *me* in the coffin and immortalize me next to Lenin?"

"You?"

"Of course. The leader's corpse does not respond to embalming so they will think of me. And they won't delay. The main thing is to tell the world that Stalin is lying next to Lenin in the mausoleum."

"Misha, these people are not murderers, are they?"

"Lelya, you don't know them! All these Berias, Malenkovs, Molotovs, and the like. You don't know these heirs of Stalin's!"

Finally, however, they did get along without me. They managed to embalm Stalin's body and bury it. And I received a pension. They summoned me before the Central Committee of the Soviet Communist party, thanked me for my past services and said:

"There will be no more films in the USSR in which Stalin participates. We will not take away your honors, awards, or your titles. You can live out your life."

A month after Stalin's death, Marshal Beria invited me for dinner at his *dacha*. He told me frankly:

"Thank God that old devil died! He wouldn't let any of us breathe. He was such a villain!"

I tried to return to Molière, Beaumarchais, Goldoni, and Shakespeare, but it was too late. Stalin was still a part of me and I still began almost every sentence with: "Is it permissible to ask . . ."

The Internationale

My Aunt Rosa said: "If the emperor dies, the empire crumbles." But she was wrong. Previously it had happened, but not this time. However, the leaders who were left in power after Stalin's death did fight it out, that's true.

Just between you and me, my Aunt Rosa considers our entire life a skirmish, as she puts it.

Right after Stalin died there was a declaration of unity and the formation of Malenkov's government, which made the world uneasy. Then Malenkov declared war on alcoholism and promised the Soviet people potatoes—plenty of potatoes—and the people even began to make up songs about potatoes.

After that, Beria was the first to burn up like a comet in the sky. That idiot left Moscow for three days in the Ukraine and the Baltic. Meantime, Malenkov came to an agreement with Khrushchev and the rest, and they decided to get rid of him. (Aunt Rosa always called Beria "the bandit from the main road.")

It was said that Beria himself was planning an overthrow and had gathered his state security troops in Moscow, since he was the minister of internal affairs in Malenkov's government. Perhaps so. In those days Marshal Konev's tanks stood in the streets of Moscow; Marshal Konev was on Malenkov's side. I was told this by Klava, who works at our cleaners, but Ephim, my neighbor in the next apartment, maintained that Marshal Konev's soldiers occupied all the railroad stations in the capital. I believed Ephim. He never lied.

Those were hot days!

According to Aunt Rosa, Beria came to the meeting of the Politburo, not suspecting anything, and then bang! He was denounced as a traitor, as an agent of the imperialists and of Tito, and so on. He pulled out a pistol, but Marshal Konev's officers disarmed him and his guards. According to the writer Klyuchnik (we are friends and tell each other everything), Beria was killed in a shoot-out when Marshal Konev's officers surrounded his *dacha*. However, Solomon the barber, whose information I never doubted, told me that Nikita Khrushchev came straight up to Beria at the Politburo meeting and planted six bullets in his neck.

The most shocking news came from a member of the circus, an illusionist named Ivan Kio. He learned that when Beria was sentenced to be shot at the trial (if indeed there was a trial), he apparently occupied himself with masturbation. Aunt Rosa told me that this "bandit from the main road" shouted out before his death: "Long live communism!" Can you imagine! He died an orthodox Leninist but was "a bandit from the main road." Aunt Rosa said: "These are the paradoxes of the times."

According to archsecret information possessed by the

apartment manager, Globa, Beria and his stooges were liquidated inside the Lubyanka prison with a machine gun. Beria and his aides were ordered into a line and told to count down—one, two, one, two, and so on. All the number twos were shot. Those who were left were told to count down again—one, two, one, two. Again, the number twos were shot. Beria was at the head of the line, so he was always number one. All the shooting took place before his eyes. When he was the last man standing, they shot him, too. (Globa told me that one of Beria's cohorts was brought to the execution on a stretcher, because he had been hospitalized with a heart attack.)

The poet and the gambler, Lado Kavsadze, who had just arrived from Soviet Georgia, told Solomon the barber that on the day of Beria's death requiems were sung in many Georgian villages. Professional mourners scratched their cheeks and howled: "An enemy of the people, Beria could not be trusted!"

Georgians had been as proud of Beria as they were of Stalin. There are those who are still proud of them.

Those were tense days! And it did not end there. Tenser days were to come.

They once called me from the party committee of the Union of Soviet Writers, of which I am a member, and told me that in two days there would be a secret party meeting of our Moscow organization of the Union of Soviet Writers at five o'clock. Nothing was said about the agenda. There was no need to mention it. Aunt Rosa called all over to say that Nikita Khrushchev had delivered his anti-Stalin speech at the Nineteenth Party Congress. The shocking details of the criminal terror "of our father and teacher," which Khrushchev included in his speech, were already known. And everybody already knew that this speech, in accordance with the decision of the Central Committee, would be read aloud at a secret party meeting, closed to nonparty members.

The party writers met at the House of Men of Letters on Vorovski Street. A party writer was one who had a party card. The rest were simply writers. Even those who had colds attended. One of our best short-story writers—I won't mention his name because he is very touchy—who was suffering from colitis, came on a motorcycle and sat by the door in case he had to leave.

Needless to say, there was full attendance. Even the buxom Gina Lollabrigida, whose movies had recently been shown at the House of Men of Letters, would not have attracted so many Soviet Shakespeares.

What amazed me was the *atmosphere*. It was half-funeral and half-wedding or birthday celebration. Many writers arrived in brand-new suits. And despite the fact that conversation was subdued, as though there were a casket in the room, the mood was one of elation. You know the feeling. It's the way it is in a theater before the curtain goes up on a comedy and everyone, even the ushers, is convinced of its success.

I personally felt as though I had won a Moskvich car in a lottery.

Only holders of party cards were granted admission to this secret meeting. As a result, only the most trusted segment of society, the Communist elite so to speak, were there. And among this elite were several legendary old men, the Bolsheviks and Leninists of the literary world. These were, of course, the victims, survivors of Stalin's rehabilitation camps somewhere in Siberia. As they walked around the room, they darted glances at Stalin's portrait, which still hung in the center of the wall, next, of course, to a portrait of our dear Lenin.

Everyone sat down. There was complete silence, except that I could hear the short-story writer's stomach growl.

In all honesty, in my many years as a party member of the Union of Soviet Writers, I could not remember such a meeting. Even the novelist Arkadi Bloh was silent and did not talk his usual nonsense.

We all expected something special. Something like the appearance of the Messiah. We were all heroes, but we were schoolboys, too. Before us loomed something great and joyous: hope! It took one's breath away to think of this. For in the course of many decades we had lost all hope and up to the last minute we did not believe in the reality of what was happening at this secret meeting. Was it really so? What if everything was a mistake? What then?

The reading of Nikita Khrushchev's address, his speech, to be more precise, lasted about five hours. Bichev-Razuvalov, the dramatist, read it. He wrote the moving play, *Dawn Over Moscow*. Bichev-Razuvalov certainly knew how to deliver a text. He read the speech as though it were a play, or a poem, or an epic. I kept wondering what it would be like performed as an operatic aria.

When Khrushchev began enumerating concrete facts about Stalin's villainy—primarily about the Great Terror—the writers broke their silence and gasps could be heard. Yes, yes, real human gasps. The writers gasped either from despair, or horror, or even joy. Perhaps everyone gasped for his own reasons. At first there were separate gasps, then a sea of gasps, and finally an ocean of gasps:

"Ooooh—aaah-uuuh . . ."

Several women writers began to cry. They were commu-

nists, but they cried nevertheless. They cried the way peasant women cry, and no one stopped them. Soon the men followed their example.

Try to picture this scene. Was it *The Last Supper?* Was it
the *Second Coming of Christ?* The old man hangs on the
wall in the full uniform of generalissimo of the USSR, and
on the platform Bichev-Razuvalov reads Khrushchev's
speech. In the back row the critic Zhen'ka Gaubitsa, with
the face of Voltaire, weeps (everyone knew that Zhen'ka
had been one of the more active stool pigeons).

If I were to be asked what I found most tragic in these
memorable five hours, I would say not Khrushchev's ex-
posure of Stalin's crimes, but the fact that all of us—"the
engineers of the human soul," the anatomists of society, in-
tellectuals, talents, all of us—had forgotten that only yesterday, in one form or another and over and over, we had
declared: "Long live the great Stalin!"

But what would have happened to us if we had not declared this?

The speech went on. No one thought of proposing a dinner break. On occasion Bichev-Razuvalov took a sip of
water and we could see that his hands were shaking. By the
way, someone once told me that this Bichev-Razuvalov,
when reading plays before acting companies, would faint,
probably to strengthen the impact of the play.

Five hours. Five hours we listened to Bichev-Razuvalov,
as though he had been to the other world and returned alive.

At the Presidium table, next to the secretary of the party
committee (whom we all called "the beard"—he wore a
pointed red beard), next to the members of the party committee and next to three most venerable writers, there sat
two characters: representatives of the Moscow Committee

and the Central Committee of the Communist party. They reminded me of mercury tubes in thermometers just before bursting. These men, of course, knew Khrushchev's speech by heart, but they sat motionless, flashing their suspicious eyes in all directions.

When the reading of the anti-Stalin speech was concluded, there was a pause. Anton Chekhov himself might have dreamed of such a pause (he was known for his theatrical pauses). But this was not an ordinary pause. No, this pause stopped the world. Not just the world. The cosmos!

We knew in advance that there would be no debate or discussion. Nevertheless, we expected something. At that crucial moment, something more should have happened. Some kind of ending. The chance to have one last accord.

Someone, pointing to the old man on the wall, shouted:

"Down with the portrait!"

Someone else shouted:

"Throw him out of the Lenin Mausoleum!"

"The beard" immediately hushed everyone up, banging his pencil against an empty glass. It was not that "the beard" or the two characters from the Moscow Committee and the Central Committee of the Communist party were fearful. Not at all, the denouncers had been too direct, too frontal, too small-minded. Naturally, no one looked at the portrait of Stalin anymore. Our Communist emotions, so to speak, had outgrown that. There was applause in the front rows. But that was not right and it soon stopped.

The "romantic" poet Ivan Ostrovoy, a powerful man with the neck of a hog, suddenly sang out:

"Arise, ye pris'ners of starvation!

Arise, ye wretched of the earth . . ."

This was the beginning sentence of our party hymm. This

was the "Internationale," known to the entire world. And that was right. There was no doubt. It was right! Everyone followed Ostrovoy's lead. And everyone stood up. More than that, everyone joined hands. More than that, everyone flung their hands in the air. At first the Presidium was at a loss, not knowing whether to take this performance as positive and supportive, or as negative, going beyond the bounds of what was permissible.

Well, this was our party anthem, this was the "Internationale." This was not "God Bless America!" So the venerable representatives of the Moscow Committee and of the Central Committeee of the Communist party were also obliged to sing. And when we came to the part about the kings, I don't think we meant only capitalists and autocrats.

When the singing was over, the Communist writers and the members of our Moscow organization began to embrace and kiss each other. There were tears in many eyes. Literary friends and literary enemies embraced each other. The scene was reminiscent of the fraternization at the end of World War I. If we had been wearing military caps, we would have tossed them in the air.

As we sauntered in groups around the hall, we spoke in clear tones, without fear, without looking over our shoulders; in short, we acted like real people. We patted each other on the shoulder. We pressed each other's hands, even though our palms were sticky—like squashed tomatoes—from tension.

The prose writer Agafonov, tall and hunched over like a question mark, laughed and asked everyone:

"What will the laureates of the Stalin Prize do with their medals now? I have accumulated eight of them. How about you?"

The literary critic and philosopher Yuli Lunaparski, black as a raven and loud as a rooster, posed a more serious question:

"What, comrades, will happen to socialist realism?"

This question hung in the air.

The journalist Boris Korolek, stocky and whistling a bit through his nose as usual, pounded himself on the chest with his fist and exclaimed:

"From this day forward everyone must try to squeeze the pus of the cult of personality out of himself!"

The idea of "squeezing" appealed to many, and Korolek received two or three cries of approval.

But neither Agafonov nor Lunaparski nor Korolek defined the general atmosphere. They were merely accessories. I felt the moment approaching when I could lay all the cards on the table, all of them. I felt we should all put on leather jackets with bullet belts, take rifles in our hands and march to the barricade to die for the revolution. I am not exaggerating. I was not alone in feeling this way. In fact, the lyric poet Romashkin, usually a shy person who speaks in a whisper and always hides his hands in his pockets, came up to me with a warlike look in his eyes.

"Do you know where they are giving out the weapons?" he asked.

He was completely serious. I told him I had also thought of weapons and barricades. We walked from the foyer together and went down to the basement level. If weapons were to be given out, it would be done at the basement level. We passed the billiard room where Ping-Pong was played and buffets served. The room had been closed that evening by special order of the management (our management fears alcohol most of all).

Weapons were not given out, however. We returned upstairs and saw several strange-looking people in the hall.
Obviously unknown, or too well known, if you know what I
mean. We call them "art critics in state uniform," or the
"elder scholars from the KGB." Which means they are sent
in case of emergency. Or to maintain order, so to speak.

At the end, an incident *did* occur. You are, of course, trying to guess what it was. It involved Arkadi Blok, that
graphomaniac who writes 600-page novels in three or four
months and calls them *Metallurgical Ode,* or *Geological
Rhapsody,* or *Cloth Trilogy.* He is completely senile and
can say what he likes.

Arkadi is of medium height, fat, with flat feet. Suddenly,
as he walked into the foyer, he jumped up on Maxim
Gorky's monument and threw his arms around Gorky's
neck.

"What is the cult of personality?" he shouted for all to
hear. "That is when one person spits on everyone else. And
what is the battle against cult of personality? That is when
everyone else spits on one person. And what is the result?
Everybody is spat upon."

The "art critics in state clothes" removed him from the
monument, properly and respectfully, and led him somewhere.

No, he was not arrested. For "the thaw" was beginning
outside. Moreover, he had been among those who sang our
party anthem, the "Internationale," that night.

As for the thaw, those were also hot days. O-o-o-o,
with a cold shower! Aunt Rosa used to say: "Nikita
Khrushchev was glorified forever because of his speech!"
And Klava from the cleaners was infuriated by the fact that

despite the thaw the speech was not printed in our newspapers. (It has still not been published.) The barber Solomon wanted personally to embrace and kiss Khrushchev because he managed to have Stalin's body removed from Lenin's Mausoleum.

To tell the truth, I was glad that, as an accompaniment to the thaw, those Malenkovs, Molotovs, and Kaganoviches were burned up like comets in the sky. "The corn grower" was better. We called Khrushchev the corn grower. He promised the people corn in addition to potatoes, and to Russian Jews he even promised corn matzo.

The prose writer Klyuchnik best characterized the period of the thaw. Even though he was not a party member, he had a brain in his head. That's a fact. He made up the following story:

"There once lived a czar, and this czar used to say that two times two is six. Everyone in his kingdom also said so. Then the czar died. The new czar said that two times two is five, and everyone was amazed. Then one learned man calculated that two times two is four and asked the new czar why he insisted that two times two is five. To this the czar answered: 'And what do you want, that two times two should again be six?' "

Perhaps because Khrushchev tried to say that two times two is five and not six, a few years later he too burned up like a comet in the sky, and we are again *basically* living according to the arithmetic of two times two is six.